Home

CLEANING &

STAIN REMOVAL

Barbara Chandler

Ward Lock Limited · London

First published in Great Britain in 1987
by Ward Lock Limited, 8 Clifford Street,
London W1X 1RB, an Egmont Company.

House editor Cheryl Brown
Designed by Anita Ruddell
Artwork by Sara Silcock

Text filmset in Baskerville No. 2
by MS Filmsetting Limited, Frome, Somerset
Printed and bound in Great Britain
by Richard Clay Ltd, Bungay, Suffolk

British Library Cataloguing in Publication Data
Chandler, Barbara
    Cleaning & stain removal.——(Home helps).
    1. Cleaning
    I. Title   II. Series
    648'.5'028   TX324

    ISBN 0–7063–6651–4

CONTENTS

INTRODUCTION

Nothing is more disheartening than spending a lot of time on a cleaning project only to find that the end result is much less than squeaky clean. And even when efforts are fully successful, it's a discouraging thought that in the fullness of time the dirt will settle and the dust will fall, the metal will tarnish and the polish dull, the glass will smear and the crumbs accumulate all over again. That's the gloomy side of things. But it is possible to take a positive attitude to cleaning and if not actually enjoy it, at least to stop it from being so tedious.

Jobs become so much easier, quicker and less tiring when you know what you're doing and stop muddling through. Knowledge of the latest cleaning products, appliances and techniques takes the sting out of many traditional chores. If you've spent a lot of time initially on creating a beautiful home, your efforts will be wasted unless you know how to maintain it. Quite simply, clean things look so much more attractive than dirty ones – and of course, they are more hygienic, too.

This book has been written in the belief that since cleaning is a task that is never going to disappear, we might as well knuckle down and find the right way of doing things, which will save money, time, effort and frustration in the long run.

Part 1 deals with general household cleaning. Chapter 1 describes the basic equipment you'll need for cleaning. The many household chemicals and cleaners available are also described, so that you can choose the best product for any job. The advice in Chapters 2, 3, and 4 will help you to tackle those everyday chores around the home from carpet stain removal to cleaning the bath; while Chapter 5 concentrates on 'spring-cleaning' tasks, those jobs which have to be tackled on a less regular basis, from cleaning the windows to polishing brass. Part 2 concentrates on the care of fabrics, from washing, drying and ironing clothes, etc., to removing stains from both washable and non-washable fabrics. Products on the market for specific cleaning tasks are mentioned throughout. If you have difficulty locating these at your local shop, a list of manufacturers' addresses is given at the end of the book.

· 1 ·

CLEANING EQUIPMENT

THE BASIC TOOLS

As with all larger, heavier tasks, the right equipment helps you to do the job quicker and better, thus saving time and temper. Keep smaller equipment together in an easy-to-carry bag or box.

☐ **Brooms and brushes**

These have soft bristles for hard floors and hard bristles for soft floors. A soft long-handled broom is an essential for sweeping wood, vinyl, cork tiles and so on, together with a dustpan and (soft) brush for transferring your sweepings to the dustbin (also good for coping with minor disasters such as spilt sugar packets and spilt soap powder). Always empty dustpan after use. An extra small brush with stiff bristles is useful for cleaning small areas of carpet, for example, to brush off dried mud. The best kinds of bristle brushes have ends which are naturally 'flagged' – that is split, to pick up the dust more easily and quickly. When buying synthetic substitutes check that the ends have been artificially 'flagged', i.e. slightly split. Stiff synthetic bristles are good for brooms which will be used outside.

Various other brushes come in handy, such as a soft bannister brush for dusting. A cobweb brush with soft head is vital in old houses with high ceilings – types are available with extending handles (Bissell and Kleeneze). Various small brushes are made for cleaning around taps, for cleaning fiddly food processors, and the insides of wine jars. A carpet whisk will reach the edges by the skirting that the vacuum cleaner may have missed. A radiator mop with flexible handle will clean behind radiators. (All from Kleeneze.) An old-fashioned feather duster is useful for carved furniture, moulded doors, etc. Shake out well after use.

There are two rules for the care of brooms and brushes:

● Store them with heads down and off the ground, to avoid flattening tufts. Some come with rings on the handle so that you can hang them on a hook: or you can add your own clip-on ring from a hardware store.

● Keep them clean. Remove fluff, etc., from tufts regularly – a wide-toothed comb is good for this. Every so often, wash the heads in warm water with a squeeze of washing-up liquid, rinse well (using cold water for bristle) and allow to dry thoroughly, heads down, off the floor, to stop water soaking into the head.

Broom handles that come away from the head as you try and do a quick sweep-up are maddening. The cheapest wooden brooms have a hole in the head into which the handle is banged. Put a little wood glue or gloss paint into the hole, and then turn the broom upside down and bang the handle into the head. You may have to shape the handle a little with a sharp knife to fit the socket. This usually works not only with new brooms, but with heads that have come adrift. Sometimes, however, you have to drive a small thin screw at an angle through the broom head downward into the handle – there is often a hole in the head for this, and you should make a starting hole in the handle with a gimlet to avoid splitting the wood. If the handle was previously nailed, remove bits with pliers and replace with a screw – saw off any split wood from handle end to provide new wood for fixing. More expensive brooms are usually fitted with sockets on handle and head that screw or lock together. Kleeneze brushes have a patented swivelling connector so that brush can be used sideways-on to clean narrow gaps.

☐ **Mops**

These are essential for lino, vinyl, cork, quarry tiles, etc., and you can even damp-mop sealed wood floors. At a pinch, a large floor cloth secured tightly with string to a broom head will do, but it is difficult to press out the water before applying it to the floor.

Many people use a sponge mop head on a handle, with built-in squeezer. Ones with larger heads do the work more quickly. Heads will last longer if you always rinse them clean at the end of a job, and allow to dry before putting away. Do not put a plastic bag over sponge head to keep it moist; this makes the sponge decay more quickly. Replace the sponge head as soon as it wears out. As with brooms, store them with heads off the floor. A dry mop needs time to soak up plenty of water before you try and squeeze out. Make sure you have a bucket large enough for your mop head. An oblong one is useful. The Vileda mop has a head of non-woven strands, and is used in a special plastic bucket with a shallow perforated section for squeezing out the water. The advantage of this design is that it leaves the floor virtually dry.

☐ **Vacuum cleaners**

Upright types have attachments for cleaning over smooth floors, but it is rather a bore to fit these on, and many people prefer to use a brush, although this will raise dust. New uprights have attachments more conveniently to hand, and some have electronic sensors to adjust power and bristle height to different surfaces. Cylinder cleaners are usually suitable for cleaning over smooth floors as well as carpets and can provide a good way of cleaning up a lot of loose dirt.

☐ **Dusters and dishcloths**

Wash dusters regularly, but separately from cloths, as traditional yellow ones are not colour fast. Make your own dusters and cleaning cloths from old towels, sheets, cotton and woollen underclothes, or from old teeshirts, etc.; but avoid non-absorbent scratchy synthetics. A soft old sock padded with other rags can make a good polishing mitt. Dishcloths can be the traditional woven type, or non-woven. Non-wovens are particularly hygienic, as they do not trap food particles. In both cases sterilize frequently in solution of household bleach. Have a separate heavy-duty floorcloth, hang to dry after use, for example over the edge of a bucket or a bowl, and sterilize often. A sponge cloth is good for mopping up liquid spills. Minky Soak-Ups absorb up to ten times their own weight in water. New Magic Touch cleaning 'Mits' are impregnated with a cleaning agent especially formulated for the various surfaces to be tackled, for example metals, furniture, glass and so on. A barrier interlining completely protects the skin from the usual cleaning grime. Minky also market a comprehensive range of impregnated cleaning cloths.

HOUSEHOLD CHEMICALS AND CLEANERS

If you get to know your way around the many cleaners and chemicals available for the care of your home, the battle is half won, for these are among your best allies. Many chemicals for cleaning and stain removal, etc., are available from chemists, hardware stores and supermarkets. However, in general it is wise to buy your chemicals wherever possible as a known branded product (even though more expensive) because the chemicals will be correctly formulated and safe for the job and the product will be safely packaged. Clear directions will be on the package, with warnings and safety precautions.

Corrosive.   *Highly flammable.*   *Toxic.*

Look out for these warning symbols on the packaging of household chemicals and cleaners. Wear rubber gloves when using them and always follow the safety notes opposite.

The chemistry of household cleaners is very complicated, and you don't have to worry too much about it, so long as you always follow directions on packs, or the safety notes on unbranded chemicals, and those given in the box below.

Briefly, acids, alkalis and solvents are all used for cleaning purposes, and stain removal. Acids cancel out or 'neutralize' the effects of alkalis and vice versa. Both strong acids and strong alkalis can be dangerous (poisonous and corrosive).

As a guide to quantities for measuring purposes bear the following in mind. A smallish sink holds about 13 litres (3 gallons) of water. An average bucket holds 9 litres (2 gallons), i.e. half a bucket is 4.5 litres (1 gallon). If you do not have a measuring jug, you can use a milk bottle to measure 1 pint (600 ml). One egg-cup equals 40 ml and one teaspoon equals 5 ml (do not use either again for food). A solution of '1 part' of a chemical to, for example, '3 parts water' means that whatever you are going to use to measure the chemical, you must use the same measure for the water, as many times as indicated.

General safety notes

● Never mix chemicals or cleaners together unless instructed.

● Keep all chemicals and cleaners clearly labelled and out of reach of children, preferably in a locked cupboard. Store upright.

● Always read carefully the warnings and directions on the pack. Even unbranded household chemicals now by law carry warning notices, if toxic, flammable, corrosive or irritant.

● Do not transfer into other containers: those which have held food or drink are particularly dangerous.

● Buy only small amounts of very poisonous or corrosive substances and safely dispose of them after use.

● Never taste or smell any chemicals if old or unidentified; throw them away and buy the product fresh.

● Store highly flammable substances, such as solvents, in a cool dark place, outside the house if possible. Keep away from flames and sparks, and never smoke when using them.

Sodium bicarbonate (baking soda or bicarb) is a mild alkali used to neutralize acid stains. You buy it as a white powder in small drums from a chemist or grocer. It cleans and deodorizes. In solution it can be used for cleaning out fridges and freezers, or for removing stains from glass and china. Undiluted, use it as a mild scouring powder. For stain removal of light fruit juice stains: sprinkle on both sides of the fabric, and moisten with water. When bubbles stop, rinse well. Don't confuse it with baking powder which is bicarb mixed with cream of tartar.

Sodium carbonate (washing soda) is a mild alkali and cleaner. It cuts grease, and comes in white crystals in packets from a hardware shop or chemist. Use it for clearing drains, and as a water softener. Add it before soap powder in hardwater areas, at a temperature of around 60°C.

Sodium hydroxide (caustic soda) is a very strong alkali available in crystals from a chemist and some hardware shops. It's very corrosive and must be handled with great care. Wear rubber gloves and don't inhale the fumes. Keep the room well ventilated and rinse accidental splashes under the running cold water tap. Always add crystals to cold water and not the other way around. For oven cleaning, you will use a branded product which will probably contain caustic soda, so be very careful and read directions on pack. Caustic soda is often recommended for drain cleaning but can react with grease to form a hard soap which blocks drains completely, so it's safest to use a branded product such as Mr Muscle.

Sodium hypochlorite (chlorine bleach) is the common household bleach sold in bottles from grocer, hardware shops, etc., under numerous brand names such as Domestos, Parazone, Brobat. It's a colourless liquid with a distinctive smell. Most bleaches on the market are between 5 and 10 per cent concentration. In practice all work equally well, although the stronger concentrations may work a little more quickly. But always follow dilution directions on pack very carefully. This bleach destroys germs and breaks up proteins in food stains and excreta. Use it neat to clean and disinfect inside and outside drains. Use diluted to whiten and disinfect dishcloths etc. (10 ml to 4.5 litres/1 gallon water). Use a solution to wash down kitchen surfaces (20 ml to 4.5 litres/1 gallon hot sudsy water) and bathroom surfaces (40 ml to 4.5 litres/1 gallon water). Use neat to clean lavatory bowls; leave it to stand overnight. Rinse lavatory brush well after using, and never mix with other lavatory cleaning powders – chlorine gas is produced and fumes can be fatal.

Use diluted in accordance with directions on bottle as an all-over bleach for white cottons, linens and most synthetics. It can also be diluted as directed (in general, 1 teaspoon to 300 ml/$\frac{1}{2}$ pint of cool water) to treat stains on these fabrics. Always rinse very thoroughly. Do not use on wool, silk or fabrics with special finishes, e.g. crease-resistant, drip dry, embossed, piqué, flameproof or showerpoof (on these fabrics you can usually use hydrogen peroxide). Beware of splashes of bleach on clothing or furnishings which will take out colours. Do not use stronger solutions than recommended on bottles as this can weaken or even destroy fabrics. Always rinse thoroughly. Never mix with other products. Do not boil chlorine bleach solutions. Undiluted or strong solutions can discolour or corrode copper, aluminium, silver and stainelss steel.

Bleach is poisonous. Wash off accidental splashes under running cold water. Do not drink. If swallowed drink plenty of cold water followed by milk and contact a doctor immediately.

Turpentine (turps) is a natural resin from pine and fir trees. It is a colourless oily liquid with a distinctive smell. Buy it from hardware or paint shops. It is a grease solvent so can be used to remove fresh grease, oil varnish and oil-based paint ('gloss and enamel') from clothes, etc. – see applying solvents by the absorbent pad method, page 77. Always launder well after using. Also use it to clean brushes after painting with oil-based paints. It is poisonous and highly flammable.

White spirit, which is a turpentine substitute, is made from a mixture of mineral oils. This colourless oily liquid can be bought from hardware or paint shops in bottles or cans. It's cheaper than turpentine and is also a grease solvent. Its uses are the same as for turpentine, above.

Methylated spirit, usually called meths, is an alcohol derived from sugar cane or wood, dyed purple with a distinctive smell. Buy it in bottles or cans from hardware and decorating shops. It's a solvent and can be used to shift marks from ballpoint and felt-tip pens, grass marks, etc. – see Stain removal chart, washable fabrics, also Carpet stain removal chart. Use neat to clean picture glass, mirrors, jewelry and piano keys. It is poisonous and highly inflammable.

Sodium pyroborate/tetraborate (laundry borax) is an alkali which cuts grease and loosens dirt and neutralizes acid stains. Buy as fine white powder from chemist or hardware shop.

For household cleaning add 10 tablespoons to a bucket of warm water for general surface cleaning and 5 tablespoons for windows. Add 1 teaspoon to washing-water to help the cleaning action of detergent – it's good for cleaning aluminium which is harmed by bicarb or washing soda.

For laundry, soak soiled cotton and linen without detergent for 30 minutes in a solution of 9 tablespoons borax to 13 litres (3 gallons) sink of warm water. For coloureds, wool and delicate fabrics, add 1 tablespoon borax per 4.5 litres (1 gallon) of warm detergent suds and wash. For the removal of fresh fruit juice, wine and tea stains on cotton and linen, spinkle the area with borax, pour boiling water through, launder and rinse.

This cleaner is very poisonous. Always keep in its original container as it is easily mistaken for icing sugar. If swallowed, give plenty of water and contact the doctor immediately. Wear rubber gloves when using cleaning or laundry solutions – borax can irritate the skin.

Household ammonia is a mild alkali sold as a liquid for household cleaning. Add 4 tablespoons to 4.5 litres (1 gallon) warm detergent solution, to clean cooker tops, tiles, etc. (Do not use on paintwork, or plastics such as vinyl floors unless removing build up of old polish.) Add 1 tablespoon for mirrors and windows. For stain removal, always test first as ammonia can take out the colour from some fabrics. Add 1 tablespoon to 600 ml (1 pint) of water or detergent solution. Allow to soak for a few minutes, then rinse well. If colour seems affected sponge immediately with white vinegar and water and rinse well. It's particularly good for perspiration stains.

Ammonia is poisonous. Always use diluted in at least 3 parts of water. Do not use with other chemicals – ammonia and chlorine bleach for example react to form a poisonous gas. Never inhale – the fumes are harmful. Wear rubber gloves and protect nose and mouth with scarf or mask if handling strong solutions. Keep the room well ventilated. Keep away from eyes, skin and clothing. Rinse small splashes immediately under running cold water. Do not drink. If swallowed give plenty of cold water and contact the doctor immediately.

Hydrogen peroxide is available as liquid in different strengths from a chemist. Common strengths are 10 vol and 20 vol, which is twice as strong. Use as a disinfectant and bleach. To use for stain removal, dilute 1 part 20 vol with 6 parts cold water and soak for 30 minutes (whites can be soaked overnight) – see Stain removal chart, washable fabrics. It's suitable for all fabrics. On strong white cottons and linens you can add a few drops direct to the stain, and watch carefully until stain disappears. Then rinse and launder immediately. To whiten yellow fabrics, e.g. woollens and silks, soak for half an hour in a solution of 1 part 20 vol with 6 parts warm water plus a few drops of ammonia. Also use for cleaning badly-stained enamel baths and lavatories. Make a paste of hydrogen peroxide and cream of tartar (from a grocer), apply to the stain and scrub hard. Rinse well and repeat if necessary.

Hydrogen peroxide is poisonous. Do not pour excess back into bottle. Do not drink. If swallowed give plenty of water and contact the doctor immediately.

Acetone is a solvent obtained from petroleum. It can be bought from a chemist. It removes nail polish, lacquers, varnishes, pitch and some paints and adhesives from body and clothes. Use on all fabrics except acetates which it dissolves. It also removes old lacquer from brass.

It's highly flammable. Only buy small quantities for immediately use. Never inhale – fumes are harmful. Keep room well ventilated. Keep away from eyes and skin.

White vinegar from a grocers, is a useful substitute for acetic acid, for stain removal. Dilute as directed. Do not use on acetate or triacetate. Ordinary malt vinegar can be used on hard water stains, e.g. shower cabinets or on stained brickwork.

Glycerine is a colourless oily liquid, with a sweet taste, buy in bottles from a chemist. Use with two parts water to lubricate old stains; also use neat to soften hands.

·2·

FLOORS & FLOOR COVERINGS

CLEANING WIPE-CLEAN FLOORINGS

Clean floors as often as you can – the longer you leave dirt the more difficult it is to shift. Wipe up spills at once – a slippery floor is very dangerous. Some substances could stain the floor if left, or even pit the surface; and people may tread the liquid to another part of the house – onto the new fitted carpet, perhaps! Always try and find out the cleaning procedures and brand names of products recommended by the flooring manufacturers. Write to the manufacturer direct, addressing your letter to the 'consumer service department'.

One advantage to living several floors up is that a lot of dirt will have dropped off feet before they enter your door; however, if you live at ground level have door mats at the front and the back. Old-fashioned door scrapers outside are a good idea, but best of all, make sure muddy shoes are taken off before entering the house. Shoe and boot storage near front and back door is a great help here. Keep a blunt knife handy for scraping off mud before storage. Remember that feet bring in not only mud but also abrasive grit which is particularly harmful to the cushioned vinyl so popular for many kitchens.

☐ **Sweeping**

Clear floors as much as possible, putting chairs up on tables, etc., rather than attempting to sweep round objects. It is usually quicker in the end, and avoids broom-bashing to legs of furniture. Sweep to a central point in the middle of the floor and then pick up all dust with dustpan and brush in one go.

☐ **Damp-mopping**

Carefully follow directions on packet. In general, for damp-mopping use a brief squirt of ordinary washing-up liquid in a bucket of warm water and have a second bucket of clean water handy to rinse off dirt as you go. Then damp-mop again with clear water to rinse. Leave undisturbed to dry.

☐ **Polishing**

Floor polishes fall into two main groups – those that are water-based and those that are solvent-based. In general, don't worry too much as long as you follow the recommendations on the polish container. But as some polishes are actually harmful to some floors (see page 15) it is useful to know the broad differences between the two types.

Water-based polishes are often called emulsions (an emulsion means that tiny particles of one liquid are suspended in another). These are 'self-shining' polishes that dry to a soft shine without any further help from you. Examples are Klear and Mansion Seel. These polishes can contain acrylics and/or synthetic wax and are suitable for most clean floors.

Before applying polish for the first time, scrub floor with a warm water and detergent solution in order to remove any grease or chemical plasticizers which may interfere with the polish. Then damp-mop with clean water and allow to dry. Apply thin coat of polish with a damp clean mop or cloth – a dry cloth soaks up too much polish. To make a useful polish applicator enclose the head of broom in a plastic bag and then wrap round a piece of old towelling and secure both firmly. This is a superior method to getting down on your hands and knees when you are then too close to your work to achieve an even layer of polish. Allow to dry for about 30 minutes and, if liked, apply a second coat a day later (you can simply re-coat heavy traffic areas if you wish). Subsequently always damp-mop before applying polish. You only need to polish every six weeks or so, and you can then damp-mop in between. However, after around five or six applications of polish you will get a polish 'build-up' – i.e. an accumulation of layers of polish which can make your floor seem dull or even discoloured. Strip the polish off, back to the original floor surface, using either a polish stripper product recommended by the polish manufacturer, or a quarter bucket (2.2 litres/$\frac{1}{2}$ gallon) of cold water to which you have added a quarter cup of cleaning powder and one cup of ammonia. Apply with sponge mop, leave five minutes, scrub then rinse.

Solvent-based polishes, primarily for wooden floors, are sometimes called spirit-based polishes, or wax polishes. They can be in the form of pastes (e.g. Mansion Wax) or in a liquid form (e.g. Johnson Traffic Wax Liquid and Antiquax Liquid Wax). Solids have a higher concentration of wax – around 30 per cent as opposed to around 10 per cent in liquids. The liquids have the advantage of cleaning away traces of dirt and old polish whilst you apply them. Solvent-based polishes should not be used on vinyl sheet or tile floors, or on cork tiles with a vinyl coating. Never apply a water-based polish to a floor previously polished with a solvent-based polish, or vice-versa.

Sweep floor before applying polish. Apply the polish with a clean dry cloth tied around a broom head, or an electric polisher.

TYPES OF WIPE-CLEAN FLOORINGS

☐ Sealed floors

Floor seals should not be confused with floor polishes. A floor seal is a semi-permanent finish applied to a scrupulously clean and smooth floor such as newly-sanded wood, unsealed cork floor or linoleum. Seals may be oleo-resinous (e.g. Bournseal) (oily) or made with polyurethanes (e.g. Ronseal). Some come in two containers which react together just before application. After sealing, floors can be simply damp-mopped or polished with either a water-based or solvent polish. Do not try to seal vinyl or waxed wood floors.

Bare wood should be sealed, unless it is kept waxed, having first been sanded clean. (If the wood is to be stained, the stain must be applied after sanding and before sealing.) Sealed wood can then be swept and damp-mopped, taking care not to over-wet. Sealer should be renewed whenever necessary, otherwise water may penetrate through floor and swell the wood fibres. Sealed floors can be polished with water-based or solvent-based polish as desired. Waxed wooden floors should be swept and then cleaned with a solvent-based liquid floor polish, which will clean at the same time as polishing.

☐ Vinyl

This can be in the form of a sheet or tiles. Sweep and damp-mop. Polish if necessary with water-based emulsion polish (e.g. Klear) – never use solvent-based polish which can destroy the surface. See damp-mopping and polishing, above. Use a little polish on a damp cloth to remove stubborn marks. A common cause of damage to cushioned vinyl is grit brought in from outside, or dragging furniture over the surface. Also beware of putting hot objects like a spare shelf from a hot oven or a hot casserole on the floor. These can cause a black scar which is impossible to remove. Take particular care with paint stripper, nail varnish remover, white spirit and paraffin – all these will harm the surface of a vinyl floor. With small spills of these, simply allow to evaporate, otherwise you may spread the damage. Mop up large spills and throw away the cloth.

☐ **Linoleum**

Do not confuse this with modern vinyls – most sheet floorings now sold are vinyl, though lino still exists in some homes, and can be specially ordered. Some new lino floors benefit from an application of oleo-resinous seal (follow manufacturer's recommendations). It is difficult to seal an old floor which has been previously polished. Damp-mop taking care not to over-wet floor, and then use either water-based or solvent-based polish. A little polish on a damp cloth should remove stubborn marks, but you can also try a gentle rub with steel wool moistened in turpentine.

☐ **Cork tiles**

It is important to find out what kind of finish has been used.

Unsealed cork tiles should be sealed (see Sealed floors, page 15). They can be then damp-mopped and polished with a water- or solvent-based polish.

Waxed cork tiles should be swept and then polished with a liquid solvent-based wax polish. A little of this polish will also remove marks.

Vinyl-coated cork tiles should be swept, damp-mopped and then polished if necessary with a water-based emulsion polish (never use a solvent-based polish).

☐ **Rubber tiles**

Sweep and damp-mop. Polish with water-based emulsion.

☐ **Ceramic tiles** (glazed ceramic)

Simply sweep and then periodically damp-mop. Do not polish. Mop up spills immediately as these make floors dangerously slippery. For unglazed tiles, see Quarry tiles, opposite.

□ **Quarry tiles** (unglazed ceramic)

These can be swept and damp-mopped, scrubbing where necessary. Use a mild liquid detergent (e.g., Stergene) not soap. For stains try Jif, white spirit or dilute bleach. For white deposits wash with neat vinegar, leave for one hour and rinse well; or BAL Ceramic Floor Cleaner which will also remove cement stains. Floors can be sealed with equal parts linseed oil/white spirit; apply sparingly. Sealed floors can be polished with solvent-based wax polish (Cardinal will restore colour).

□ **Brick floors**

During cleaning keep the floor as dry as possible. Sweep, then scrub with a solution of washing-up liquid and warm water, using a cleaning powder such as Flash if heavily soiled. But avoid soap, which could cause white crystals. Rinse over with clear water and then mop as dry as possible. You can buy special sealers for stone and brick.

□ **Stone and slate**

These can be sealed with special sealers such as Belsealer from A. Bell. They can be swept and damp-mopped, and polished if sealed with a solvent-based liquid wax polish.

□ **Marble**

Sweep and damp-mop. Wipe up fats and oils immediately using a damp cloth with a little washing-up liquid.

CARPETS

Carpet cleaning methods on the whole are the same for wool and synthetic carpets. However, note that wool can absorb relatively large amounts of water without seeming damp. Its natural moisture content is 15 to 18 per cent of its own weight and it can retain up to 40 per cent of moisture without becoming saturated. Synthetic fibres absorb much less water than wool: under normal conditions, for example, polypropylene might have a moisture content of only 1 per cent of its own weight. It is important therefore when cleaning synthetics to use less water than for wool. Otherwise excess water which cannot be absorbed by the fibre may run down into the carpet backing and in the long term cause 'cellulosic browning'. Brown stains from the carpet backing fibres work their way up through the damp pile to the surface of the carpet, and require professional treatment for removal.

Wool carpets respond adversely to some chemicals used in stain removal treatments. Solutions of ammonia for example should be very weak and only used after thorough testing as they may cause colour changes. Household bleach can cause wool fibres to disintegrate.

You are less likely to have problems with static electricity shocks with wool than with synthetic due to the higher moisture content of wool. This problem appears to vary from one person to another. If your family seems badly affected, first try increasing the moisture content of your room with plants or humidifiers. Severe cases can be professionally treated by a trade carpet cleaner, but before the anti-static treatment can be administered, the carpet must be spotlessly clean. Pet hairs may be particularly difficult to dislodge. For small areas wide sticky tape is effective. Otherwise try wiping over with a barely damp sponge.

If you have inherited a carpet and are not sure of its fibre obtain a small fibre sample from an out-of-the-way spot. Hold this very close to the flame of a burning match. Wool burns with difficulty with a small flickering flame, and a strong smell of burning hair. The ash that is formed is easily crushed between the fingers. Nylon melts, smelling rather like sealing wax, and producing a very hard deposit which is difficult to break with the fingers. Acrylics shrivel away from the flame, and form small black beads. Polypropylene fibres will burn, but soon shrink away from the flame and go out.

When buying a new carpet ask for care advice from the shop. It is also worth obtaining the manufacturer's name and address and writing away for any specific care labels or leaflets they may publish. Correct fitting makes a carpet easier to keep clean and it is usually worth while paying for a professional carpet fitter.

The Carpet Cleaners Association advise against vigorous brushing or excessive vacuum cleaning of a new carpet, nor should a new carpet be shampooed. Some new carpets tend to show a fair amount of fluff; this is quite normal and can best be removed gently with a carpet sweeper. A few single tufts or loose ends may stand above the pile. Never try to pull these out, but simply cut them level with a small pair of sharp scissors. The pile of a carpet lies naturally in one direction like a cat's fur and when new the colour will seem completely even. But as the carpet receives wear the pile becomes disturbed, creating light and dark patches. This, too is normal, and most people find it quite acceptable. 'Shading', as it is called, is minimized if you buy a carpet with a twist pile.

☐ **Vacuum cleaning**

Dirt and grit embedded in the pile of a carpet will not only dull its appearance but also shorten its life. Your protection against this is regular vacuum cleaning – at least once a week and up to three times a week over traffic lanes and in heavily used rooms. Basically, vacuum cleaners fall into two types: upright cleaners with rotating beater bars and cylinder cleaners with a hose attachment that works mainly on suction only. New cylinder models, however, may incorporate a beating action and a 'power boosting' facility. For traditional cut-pile carpets, a beating action is recommended because it loosens and removes soil deep within the pile, and at the same time 'grooms' the tufts into their original upright position. It is not true that the beater bars wear the carpet out; it is the grit that they dislodge which will shorten a carpet's life. Upright cleaners are available which can be adjusted to suit the depth of the carpet's pile.

Undoubtedly, however, cylinder vacuum cleaners are lighter and easier to move around than their upright counterparts – indeed some new models can even be hand-held. They are also more suitable for carpets with really long piles ('shags') and also for loop pile carpets. You can often use this type of cleaner for adjoining areas of smooth flooring. After vacuuming, long-pile carpets will benefit from a special tool called a carpet rake, which looks a bit like an autumn leaf collector, but makes a good job of fluffing up the pile. Buy one from a specialist carpet shop.

Depending upon the make of vacuum cleaner, reaching the edges of the room may be a problem. Many uprights now clean right up to the skirting board, and most cylinders have a special crevice tool which enables you to tackle the dust-trap between floor and skirting. However, if you do have a narrow band of dust around a room's perimeter, use either a stiff brush called a whisk or a damp sponge to clean it away. Try and protect your carpet at its most vulnerable points. Put down rugs or matching pieces of carpet in front of the settee, for example, where people sit and watch TV and grind their heels into the carpet. Similarly protect the area in front of a fireplace, under a kneehole desk, by the front door and by the door to the kitchen. Use a guard in front of the fire.

Deodorizing powders with a masking scent are now popular. Sprinkled over the carpet before vacuuming they dispel unpleasant smells such as cigarette and food odours. These powders, however, do not have a cleaning action. But a new carpet cleaning powder called Sapur has recently come on to the market which releases dirt and then binds it together so that it can be vacuumed easily.

▶ *Floors & Floor Coverings*

Even if you possess a vacuum cleaner, a carpet sweeper is a useful additional household tool. Ideal for the quick clean up (no flex to plug in) a sweeper will pick up threads, crumbs, fluff and so on, but will not dislodge ingrained dirt. Light and easy to move around, sweepers are ideal for the elderly or the disabled. Lightweight cordless rechargeable vacuum cleaners are now also available.

☐ Carpet shampooing

After a while, you may find that your carpet is looking dull and wet cleaning becomes desirable. This could happen perhaps once or twice a year. Take a clean white cloth and dampen it slightly; rub it over your carpet. Heavy soiling indicates that wet cleaning is required. You can shampoo a carpet yourself at home, or you can call in a professional, making sure that the operator is a member of a reputable trade organization.

There are two main methods of carpet shampooing, both of which can be carried out either by you at home (with hired equipment if necessary) or by a professional. The first is referred to as the *dry foam method*, because the foamy shampoo used dries to fine powdery crystals which are vacuumed up along with surface dirt. However, this method does not penetrate deep into the pile. The second method called *hot water extraction* forces hot water and cleaner deep into the pile and then sucks it out again in a single action, leaving the carpet dry within about one hour.

For the dry foam method, always use a quality branded shampoo such as Bissell or 1001. Never use household detergent or any shampoos which smell of ammonia. Follow instructions exactly. First test for colourfastness, by rubbing a small out-of-the-way patch of carpet with a cloth wetted with the shampoo solution. If colours of patterned carpets appear to run, call in a professional cleaner. Plain carpets may transfer a little of their colour to the cloth, but the effect of this should not be noticeable and you can still proceed with the shampooing.

You can apply shampoo by hand using a sponge or small brush, but there is a danger of making the carpet too wet which could lead to shrinkage, staining, mildew and/or rot, and it is difficult to distribute the shampoo evenly. Preferably, buy or borrow a carpet shampooer. Some wet-and-dry vacuum cleaners now have a shampoo facility. Electric shampoo machines can be hired from many hardware stores. Electric machines are the best choice for medium pile carpets, but take extra care with shag piles as the pile can become tangled in some machines. Apply the shampoo, leave to dry (6–8 hours), then vacuum thoroughly.

Floors & Floor Coverings ▶

For the hot water extraction method, Professional cleaning is advisable if your carpet is badly soiled, flattened, stained, flooded or has colours which are likely to run. Professionals may use a shampoo system, or they may offer 'hot water extraction'. These machines are also now available for home hire, from dry-cleaners such as Sketchley. Follow directions; do not exceed temperatures recommended, and stick very carefully to the concentration of cleaning solution specified.

Rugs and carpets can also be taken away for factory dry cleaning – indeed this is essential for oriental carpets which should not be wet cleaned.

☐ Removing carpet stains

Note These methods can also be used with caution on upholstery (see page 30) substituting a solution of upholstery shampoo.

Some professional cleaning companies such as ServiceMaster can supply you with a small stain removal kit for emergency action in between professional cleaning or you can make up your own kit as detailed below. Try and keep the solutions in one place with directions.

General safety notes

- Keep all chemicals out of the reach of children.
- Never use bottles which have held drinks to hold solutions.
- Many chemicals are flammable. Do not smoke whilst using them.
- Always work in a well-ventilated room.

☐ Stain removal kit

1 Make up a solution of a branded carpet shampoo of the dry foam type. Do not be tempted to use washing-up liquid which simply re-attracts dirt.

2 Make up a solution of laundry detergent (preferably of the enzyme type): dissolve 1 teaspoon in 300 ml ($\frac{1}{2}$ pt) of warm water.

3 You can add to the above solutions 1 teaspoon of white vinegar if carpet colours do not appear fast when testing. Re-test before proceeding.

4 A branded solvent for grease and stain removal, obtainable in bottles from chemist, hardware or department store, e.g. Beaucaire, Thawpit or Dabitoff. **Caution**: flammable. You must always use solvents of this kind on *perfectly dry carpets*.

5 An ammonia solution made up of 1 tablespoon of household ammonia to 1 cup of water. Test carefully before using on wool, as dyes may not prove fast. Avoid inhaling the fumes which may irritate the lungs.

6 Methylated spirits, from a chemist, hardware or DIY shop. **Caution**: flammable.

7 Acetone, which you can buy in a small bottle from a chemist. Nail varnish remover is generally acetone-based but usually contains oil to condition the nails. Acetone is therefore preferable, but it is very flammable.

8 Also keep handy clean white tissue or kitchen roll, a small clean sponge, and a small spoon or a blunt knife or a clean spatula or lolly stick.

If your attempts at stain removal are not entirely successful you can always resort to camouflage; place a rug, or a pot plant over the damage, or as a last resort make a patch.

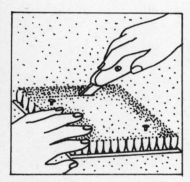

Patching a fitted carpet using a spare offcut or hidden piece from under the furniture. Top left *For an exact fit, cut through the patch and the stained area together. Remove the damaged piece. Smear Copydex on the edges of the hole and the patch.* Bottom left *Line the hole with paper, cut larger than the patch. Lay a piece of hessian on top and apply adhesive to it.* Bottom right *Insert patch and tap around the edges with a hammer.*

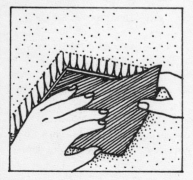

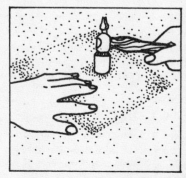

CARPET STAIN REMOVAL A–Z

Adhesives Quick action is essential. Many adhesives are impossible to remove once dry, although you may be able to snip away the top of the affected fibres. In general, scrape off excess, and then repeatedly dab with detergent solution, so as to avoid spreading the damage. *Clear household adhesives*: remove with meths before set, or try acetone. *Epoxy resins :* use meths before set – once set virtually impossible to remove. *Latex*: wipe off with damp cloth before set; otherwise write to makers for special solvent. *PVA wood glues*: remove with damp cloth before set. *Contact adhesives*: remove with meths before set, or try acetone.

Ballpoint Dab stain with meths, then with carpet shampoo solution.

Beer/Lager Blot up with clean tissues or cloth as much of spillage as possible. Then dab repeatedly with carpet shampoo solution. Allow to dry. Treat any remaining marks with a stain removal solvent. If an old stain, try meths, followed by carpet shampoo solution.

Bicycle oil See grease.

Blood Use a stiff brush to remove any hard deposits. Blot well with clear cold water and tissues. If stain persists, add a few drops of ammonia to the water, which will give the stain a foamy appearance. Continue blotting until stain disappears, and then rinse and blot repeatedly with cold clean water. For residual marks apply laundry detergent solution, using enzyme detergent. Leave this to stand on the stain for half an hour before rinsing and blotting off.

Candlewax Pick away as much as you can of the hardened deposits. Lay blotting or brown paper over the stain and gently dab with tip of a hot iron, frequently moving the paper so that it can soak up the melted wax. Finish off with a stain removal solvent and treat any traces of colour from dyes with meths. (See diagram on page 24.)

Chewing gum Pick off as much as you can, breaking up the gum surface with the edge of a blunt knife or similar. Carpet specialists sometimes sell a special aerosol for treating gum stains, otherwise try freezing with ice cubes contained in plastic bag, and then picking off the pieces. Finally apply cleaning solvent.

Chocolate Pick off as much as possible, then dab with carpet shampoo solution. When dry, if stain persists, use stain removal solvent.

Cocoa Sponge stain gently with clean warm water, then a solution of carpet shampoo. Allow to dry completely and then apply stain removal solvent to remains of stain.

Coffee   Treat as quickly as possible as this can be a particularly tricky stain to remove. Blot up as much of excess as possible with clean tissues or cloth, then sponge with warm water and blot again with tissues. Apply a solution of carpet shampoo, and allow stained area to dry completely. Remove any lingering traces of stain with stain removal solvent.

Cooking oils   See grease.

Cream   Sponge with carpet shampoo solution and allow to dry completely. Then use a branded stain removal solvent for any lingering traces of grease.

Curry   This is a notoriously difficult stain to remove and you may have to call in a professional cleaner. However, acting immediately you can try the following: remove any deposits and then dab stain lightly with 1 tablespoon of laundry borax dissolved in 600 ml (1 pint) of warm water. Then rub a little glycerine into the pile and leave for around 10 minutes to soften stain. Sponge with a solution of laundry detergent. Finally blot out well with warm water followed by clean dry tissues.

Dyes   Methylated spirits will remove most colouring matters but old stains may need softening with a mixture of equal parts of glycerine with warm water.

Egg   Scrape and blot up excess. Then apply a solution of carpet shampoo. You can use an ammonia solution on synthetics but test very thoroughly before using on wool.

Fats   See grease.

Felt-tip pens   Dab with methylated spirits, blotting well. Follow with carpet shampoo solution.

Floor wax   Treat as for candlewax (see diagram below). Finish off by applying a branded stain removal solvent.

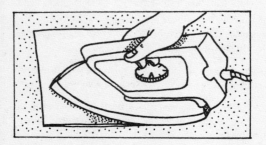

To remove candlewax or floorwax from a carpet, lay blotting or brown paper over the stain and gently dab with the tip of a hot iron.

Foods In general, act as soon as you can, scrape off excess and then sponge over with carpet shampoo solution. Allow to dry completely, then remove any grease stains with stain removal solvent. See also separate entries under specific food stains.

Fruit juice Blot up excess, then sponge over with clean warm water. Apply a carpet shampoo solution, then a laundry detergent solution. If stain persists you can try an ammonia solution, but test very well before using this on wool. Methylated spirits may be effective on any lingering traces of colour, or you can try a few drops of hydrogen peroxide (be sure to test first).

Furniture polish Treat wax polishes as for candlewax. Use a stain removal solvent, then a carpet shampoo solution.

Gravy/Sauces Scrape up and blot up excess, then sponge over with clean warm water. Apply a solution of carpet shampoo. Allow to dry completely, then treat remaining stain with stain removal solvent.

Grease/Oils/Fats These stains should respond well to a branded stain removal solvent, making sure you work from outside of stain inwards and blotting repeatedly to absorb the loosened grease. Follow with an application of carpet shampoo solution. Often the stain reappears after a short while. This is because it is difficult to treat the base of the pile and the stain 'wicks' its way up to the surface. Re-treat as many times as necessary.

Ice-cream Use method as for chocolate.

Ink (permanent) Blot up excess with clean tissues and apply laundry detergent solution (work from outside of stain in). After thorough testing, try bleaching with hydrogen peroxide plus a few drops of ammonia.

Ink (washable) Blot up excess with clean tissues. Then sponge over with a solution of laundry detergent repeating blotting.

Iron mould (rust) Very difficult to remove without special chemicals: you may need to call a professional cleaner. You can try a branded stain removal solvent, followed by a carpet shampoo solution.

Jam/Marmalade See foods. Any traces of colour stains may respond to methylated spirits, or to bleaching with hydrogen peroxide, but test first.

Ketchup As for gravy, but if colour persists try bleaching with hydrogen peroxide (after testing).

Lipsticks/Blushers   Treat with a branded stain removal solution. Use methylated spirits on any remaining traces of colour.

Lotions   If greasy, treat as described under grease. If non-greasy use methods described under spirits. (See diagram on page 24.)

Mascara   Carefully blot up to absorb excess, making sure you do not spread the stain. Then use a branded stain removal solvent working from the outside of the stain in. An ammonia solution may be effective, but test very thoroughly first.

Medicines   Blot well to absorb excess, then sponge with warm water. If stain persists, apply a branded stain removal solvent, and use methylated spirits on lingering traces of colour.

Metal polish   Use a branded stain removal solvent, then a carpet shampoo solution.

Mildew   First of all, work out why carpet went mouldy and cure the cause of the damp otherwise the stain will simply happen again. Try sponging with carpet shampoo solution, then a laundry detergent solution. Try bleaching bad stains with hydrogen peroxide but test well first.

Milk   Blot up excess quickly and work hard to remove remaining traces which can turn rancid and smell. Sponge with clean warm water blotting well, then apply a carpet shampoo solution. If this is not fully effective use an ammonia solution, but test well first.

Mud   Very carefully pick off any loose fragments, leaving any wet deposits to dry. Then vacuum or brush off with a stiff clean carpet brush. If marks persist, sponge gently with carpet shampoo solution.

Mustard   Use a solution of carpet shampoo.

Nail varnish   Preferably use acetone, but failing this apply nail varnish remover. If stain persists, follow with stain removal solvent.

Ointments   Treat as for grease and use meths on any lingering traces of colour.

Paint   Old dried stains are often impossible for the amateur to shift and it is wisest to call in a professional cleaner. *Emulsion paints* (including vinyls) are water-based. If you act quickly you can remove all traces of a fresh stain by repeated sponging with cold water, provided you keep the stain damp. Finish off with an application of carpet shampoo solution. Dried stains can sometimes be picked off with the fingernails, and any last traces snipped away with a sharp pair of scissors. You can try an application of white spirit or turpentine which should be left to soften the stain. Blot well and then apply carpet shampoo solution. *Gloss paint* is oil-based, and fresh stains can be removed with turpentine/white spirit, as long as treatment is immediate. Blot repeatedly, taking care not to spread stain. Follow with an application of branded stain removal solvent, then carpet shampoo solution. Dried stains are virtually irremovable: try carefully snipping away the affected fibres, the stain may simply be sitting on the very top of the carpet. Otherwise consider making a patch.

Rust   See iron mould.

Salad cream   Use a solution of carpet shampoo, blotting well. When dry apply a stain removal solvent.

Salt   Vacuum up as soon as possible because when left in the pile it absorbs moisture, attracts dirt and possibly affects carpet colourings.

Scorch marks   Trim slight burns with scissors; on heavier marks charred fibres can be removed with a wire brush and coarse sand paper. Use gently circular movements. You may find that a patch is necessary (see diagram on page 22).

Shoe polish   Use a branded stain removal solvent, taking care not to spread the stain. Follow with a solution of carpet shampoo. If the stain persists try an ammonia solution but test first.

Soft drinks   See fruit juices.

Soot   Vacuum carefully and gently and avoid rubbing the soot in. With an upright cleaner try using the upholstery tool. Then apply a solution of carpet shampoo.

Spirits   Sprinkle with an absorbent powder (talc or fuller's earth) to stop the stain spreading, then blot up with clean tissues. Squirt with soda syphon or sponge with clear warm water. Apply carpet shampoo solution, then a solution of laundry detergent. Blot well with clean warm water. If traces of colour remain, try methylated spirits, or a few drops of hydrogen peroxide (but test first).

Tar   Very carefully scrape up as much as you can, making sure that you do not spread the stain. Then, working from outside in (as always) apply a branded stain removal solvent, blotting frequently to absorb loosened deposits. Obstinate stains may respond better if you first soften them with neat eucalyptus oil, or a glycerine solution (equal parts of glycerine and warm water).

Tea Act as quickly as you can, blotting up as much as possible. Flush with a squirt from a soda syphon or sponge with clean warm water. Follow with a carpet shampoo solution and allow to dry. If grease stains persist, apply a branded stain removal solvent. Dried stains can be treated with laundry borax solution using 1 tablespoon to 600 ml (1 pint) of warm water. On obstinate marks, soften with a glycerine solution, leave for one hour then sponge off with clear warm water and apply a solution of carpet shampoo.

Urine You must treat these stains at once. Old stains will require professional treatment and even this may not succeed on some fibres. Blot up as much as you can then flush with squirt from a soda syphon. Sponge with carpet solution adding a few drops of antiseptic or household disinfectant. Sponge and blot repeatedly, and finish with several applications of cold water.

Vomit Very gently scrape up all solids and blot up liquids taking care not to rub anything into the carpet. Sponge gently with carpet shampoo solution to which you have added a few drops of antiseptic or household disinfectant. If stain persists sponge with a laundry detergent solution. You can also try an ammonia solution, but test first.

Wine Sprinkle with an absorbent powder (talc or fuller's earth) to prevent stain spreading, then blot up excess. Sponge with clean warm water and apply a solution of laundry detergent. If stains persist, try bleach with a few drops of hydrogen peroxide, but test first.

RUGS

Contrary to popular belief, rugs should not be taken up and beaten over a line as this can loosen the fringe or hem and could even lead to a breakdown of the weave and/or fibres in time. Use a vacuum cleaner or carpet sweeper in the normal fashion, except for fur rugs, see below. From time to time, turn the rug over and vacuum clean the back. Occasionally, on a fine day, you can lay your rugs face down and flat on dry grass and gently beat the back.

There are so many different types of rugs now available for the home that it is difficult to give general advice. Where possible, try and keep carefully any care instructions that come with the rug. Some rugs are washable, for example long pile cottons and acrylics, and some 'flokati' white wool rugs from Greece. Wash by hand: the bath makes a suitable large container and preferably use a spin drier to absorb excess moisture. Dry over two lines if possible, to support the weight. When dry, raise the pile with a stiff clean brush.

Plains and patterned Those made in a similar fashion to carpets, and some kelims, can be shampooed occasionally using the same methods as described for carpets, and dried flat.

Rugs from abroad These include orientals, dhurries and numdah embroidered felts and cannot be washed or shampooed, but must be dry cleaned. Many professional dry cleaners can cope with dhurries and numdahs but orientals of any value should go to a specialist carpet cleaner.

Fur rugs In general avoid using a vacuum cleaner and instead shake outside from time to time, and occasionally lay face down on old sheet and gently beat the back. Some rugs without a backing can be gently shampooed with carpet shampoo and a sponge. Try not to wet the skin. Rugs with a backing can be sprinkled with fuller's earth or warm bran which should be left for a few hours then brushed out using a clean stiffish brush.

Mattings Commonest types are made of rush: these should be vacuumed in the normal fashion, but every so often should be lifted to sweep or vacuum dirt that has collected underneath. Dirty matting can be sponged or scrubbed with a solution of warm water and washing up liquid: greasy marks can be removed with a solution of warm water and washing soda. Matting can be dried with a fan heater or hair-drier, on low setting at a minimum distance of 30 cm (1 ft).

·3·

FURNITURE & BEDDING

UPHOLSTERED FURNITURE

Vacuum or brush regularly, because dirt and dust shorten the life of the fabric and will dull colours. But do not use a stiff brush, which will damage the fabric. To remove pet hairs, lint, etc., use a barely-damp sponge or wide sticky tape.

Turn reversible cushions regularly to restore shape and springiness. Plump up cushions with loose fillings. Zipped covers do not necessarily mean that the covers can be washed, or even dry-cleaned. They are for the manufacturer's convenience, not yours.

Try and keep upholstery away from prolonged sunlight and heat. Ideally place your upholstery out of the sun; in bright sunlight, draw the blind or the curtains. Avoid placing upholstery close to fires or radiators. You can use slip-covers to protect arms and backs of chairs and settees.

Always treat spots and spills immediately. Scrape off any solids with blunt knife or spoon. Blot up any liquids gently with *white* paper tissues, kitchen paper or clean absorbent cloth. Do not rub stain in. In general you can follow the spot removal techniques under Removing carpet stains, page 21, substituting an upholstery shampoo for a carpet shampoo solution. Work from edges of spot inwards. Work with minimum amounts of cleaner and blot well between applications. But spot removal on upholstery is notoriously difficult due to the complications of interlinings, paddings etc. So always test first on an out-of-sight-area. If colours come away on cleaning cloths or change or run into each other, call in a professional cleaner.

When necessary (two or three times a year) shampoo upholstery, using branded upholstery shampoo and manufacturer's applicator. Carefully follow manufacturer's instructions. Shampoo before upholstery gets very dirty. Shampooing is safe for most cotton, wool, linen and synthetic fabrics (e.g. Dralon velvets, polypropylenes). Professional cleaners should treat suede, silk, stain, velvets (with the exception of acrylics, such as Dralon), brocades and all very delicate coverings. Vacuum upholstery before and after shampooing; do not over-wet or you can harm paddings or backings (e.g. Dralon cotton backing can shrink).

☐ Leather upholstery

Test to see if it is 'treated' (lacquered) or untreated. (Most modern furniture is treated but some imported styles are not.) Rub an out-of-sight part with soap on a damp cloth. If colour comes off, or a mark is left, your leather is untreated.

For treated leather   Wash with warm water and solution of soap flakes (Lux) or good toilet soap (preferably a pure soap with glycerine). Do not use household detergents (which weaken the finish) or laundry soap (which is too alkaline). Do not over-wet as this damages stitching and padding. You can use a soft nail brush if necessary. Sponge with clean warm water. Feed every so often with branded leatherfood, e.g. Hidelife from Bridge of Weir.

For untreated leather   Sponge greasy marks with a little white spirit on a soft cloth. Then use soap and water as above, but only barely wet the surface. Treat oily stains (e.g. spilt food) with rubber solution (from a cycle repair repair kit). Squeeze solution over mark and allow to dry for twenty-four hours. Roll it off: it absorbs all or most of the oil. On no account, apply leatherfood to untreated leather.

Scratches and scuffing on leather can be touched up with a coloured lacquer. Or try matching the colour as near as you possibly can with a shoe dye or even a felt-tip pen! You won't notice from a distance.

☐ Suede upholstery

This should be professionally cleaned, but you may be able to remove some marks with SwadeAid and SwadeGroom sold for cleaning coats. You can give initial all-over protection with Swade Guard Spray.

☐ Vinyl covered upholstery

In general, simply dust, or wipe over with cloth or sponge well wrung out in solution of warm water and soap flakes. Then wipe over with clear water and dry off with soft cloth. If very soiled, buy a special vinyl upholstery cleaner from a car accessory shop. Ballpoint pen ink is particularly difficult to remove; this suggested method came from Parker Inks:

1 Moisten clean cloth or tissue with alkaline, alcoholic soap solution (Lin:Saponis Meth:) from a chemist.

2 Rub in direction of mark, changing to fresh part of cloth until no further stain is picked up on cloth.

3 Repeat process, using a paste made with warm water, and a bar of household soap (Fairy or Sunlight) cut in slivers.

4 Rub with damp clean cloth dipped in scouring powder.

5 Use soap again if necessary.

6 Rinse with clean water.

LOOSE COVERS

Covers of heavy fabrics such as velvets and velours should be dry cleaned. Test other covers for colourfastness (see page 66), if not fast they should also be dry cleaned.

Most covers however, can be washed. Before taking off, inspect for small tears, holes, etc. Take covers off carefully and mend these. Then brush well outside to remove loose dirt, paying particular attention to dirt-attracting crevices around seams, pipings, pleats, etc. Or run a vacuum cleaner attachment over covers before removing.

Wash by machine provided you have care instructions which advise this. Otherwise, using solution of warm water and mild detergent (e.g. Dreft, Stergene), squeeze covers through gently by hand. Wash for a second time if covers seem very dirty. Rinse three times, and spin for one minute or wring. Hang to dry, if possible between two lines so that air can get into folds of the fabric.

Iron when slightly damp, on wrong side for a matt finish, on right side for a shiny one. Iron back and seat and sides lightly, and then iron any pleats or frills very carefully and put cover back on chair. Then finish off ironing back and seat and sides. Many cotton and linen covers may be improved by a light starching; in which case, allow covers to dry completely and then sprinkle with warm water before ironing. But do not starch if fabric is crease-resistant or glazed, or has any other special finish. Fabrics with special finishes are best drip-dried.

Washed gently and carefully as above, covers should not shrink. But if they do, re-wet in warm water and allow to dry for only a short while. Then stretch covers back on chair while very damp, and press with iron till dry, in position.

Stretch covers can usually be machine-washed and need no ironing.

'CABINET' FURNITURE

(Wooden chests, cupboards etc.)

☐ Modern furniture

Regular dusting, always along the direction of the grain and without circular movements, should be sufficient. Use a soft old paintbrush, or baby's hairbrush to get dust out of mouldings and carvings. Check maker's recommendations. Use a damp cloth and detergent solution if necessary. Rinse and buff to a shine with a dry, clean soft cloth. Occasionally, you can use an aerosol or trigger polish (Sparkle, Mr Sheen). Modern teak furniture in particular only needs dusting. Special teak oils are available but should be used *very sparingly* only two or three times a year. Otherwise you will do more harm than good.

☐ Old furniture

Apply a good wax polish sparingly (cream, paste, trigger or aerosol). Revive dull finishes with Antiquax Wood Restorer. It is not true that the excellent cream polishes containing silicone will harm antiques.

Always put table mats under hot plates and dishes. Get professional treatment for marks and stains on valuable or antique furniture.

Use the methods below with caution, particularly on veneered surfaces.

Scratches and stains   Always try remedies in an inconspicuous area first. An application of wax polish rubbed hard with a finger will hide many small blemishes or you can try rubbing with the cut kernel of a brazil nut or a little linseed oil on a clean cloth. Or you can use a special wax crayon by Liberon, who have an excellent range of products for wood restoration and care. Or try Topps Scratch Cover (light, medium or dark shades) from a hardware or DIY shop. For deep scratches, use a coloured wood stopping.

Rings and marks   White heat marks and alcohol stains may respond to rubbing with metal polish; wipe immediately with a clean cloth. Or try a paste of cigarette ash and olive oil or Topps Ring Away. Always rub in the direction of grain and proceed with caution.

Slight burn marks   Rub off burnt material with very fine glass paper; then use turpentine to soften surrounding finish and try to spread it over damaged area before re-polishing.

Ink stains are very difficult to remove. Try dabbing stain with

Furniture & Bedding

household bleach on cotton wool, but do not rub. Blot well after each application. For severe or extensive marks, buy wood bleach, e.g. Rustins.

CANE FURNITURE

Brush to remove dirt and dust. For awkward crevices, use a vacuum cleaner attachment, or blow out dust with a hair-dryer. Very dirty cane can be sponged with warm water and a little washing soda. Do not over-wet and wipe off with clear water. Allow to dry naturally away from heat. Varnished cane can be wiped with a damp cloth.

BAMBOO FURNITURE

This can be dusted as above. You can use an aerosol or trigger cleaner such as Sparkle or Mr Sheen. When very dirty, sponge with a solution of warm water and soap flakes, plus one teaspoon of laundry borax from a chemist. Then wipe over with warm salted water and allow to dry naturally (if possible, outside on a fine day).

PLASTIC FURNITURE

This should not be dry dusted as grit can scratch. Wipe with warm water plus a squeeze of washing-up liquid, then rinse off and rub to shine with soft dry cloth. Or use aerosol or trigger cleaner/polish. Avoid abrasives of any kind including cream cleaners. Treat scratches by rubbing with metal polish.

CHROME FURNITURE

A rub with a damp cloth should usually be sufficient. Rub a little bicarbonate of soda on stubborn marks. If chrome is pitted treat with cleaner from a car accessory shop.

BEDS AND BEDDING

After buying a new bed always remove completely any plastic wrappers. Once a week for the first month turn the mattress over or swing it round on the bed to reverse the head and foot ends (unless made of foam: foam mattresses must not be turned). After this try and turn at least every three months. Every few months, clean mattress and upholster base carefully with a soft brush to remove dust and fluff.

□ **Spills and accidents**

Act quickly to avoid wetting the upholstery filling and to prevent the stain drying.

1 Strip off bedclothes and stand mattress on its side.

2 Blot up any liquids with an absorbent cloth, old towel or plain paper towels.

3 Immediate sponging with cold water clears many liquid stains. Don't worry about leaving a small water mark; it won't show when the bed is made. It is more important to get rid of any smell. Avoid over-wetting by blotting as you work.

Hot-water bottle leaks and flood damage   Use a hair dryer to dry off mattress; for large areas, protect the floor and support the matress safely (lengthwise, on its edge) in front of a carefully positioned fan heater (but not a radiant heater). Inspect frequently. Hang up bedclothes to dry.

Tea, coffee and milk-based drinks   Sponge with warm borax solution of 1 teaspoon laundry borax to 300 ml ($\frac{1}{2}$ pint) of water, then sponge with clear water. When this is dry, an aerosol branded stain-removal solvent, e.g. Goddard's Dry Clean, should clear any grease but use sparingly on a foam mattress. Brush the cover lightly but thoroughly to clear the deposit.

Urine   Sponge with a warm solution of mild synthetic (i.e. soapless) detergent or upholstery shampoo, and then wipe with cold water plus a few drops of antiseptic, e.g. Milton or Dettol.

Vomit and diarrhoea   Scoop up solid matter with a spoon, try not to spread the stain. Then, using a sponge or soft nail brush, treat as for urine above. When the section is as clean as possible, wipe with cold water plus antiseptic as above.

Blood   Sponge with cold salt water and then with clear cold water. An upholstery cleaner, suitable for blood stains, is usually effective on fresh marks and may clear dried stains.

□ **Continental quilts (duvets)**

Follow carefully any care labels on your quilt or quilt packaging. Always use quilts with washable covers.

Quilts with synthetic fillings can be washed in the bath. Knead gently in warm soapy water, rinse well, and squeeze dry. Hang well-supported on two parallel lines.

Down and feather-and-down quilts will benefit from an occasional shaking out of doors on a fine day. Have these quilts professionally cleaned when necessary, never use a coin-operated dry cleaning machine – your quilt could harbour dangerous fumes.

For spills remove the cover gently. Push the filling away from stained area, then gently sponge with warm soapy water, then with clear water, taking care not to wet the filling.

☐ **Blankets**

It is usually easier to have blankets dry-cleaned. If you use a coin-op machine, be sure to air thoroughly before use. If you want to wash blankets follow carefully any manufacturer's directions and work according to fibre.

For machine-washable blankets Make sure your washing machine or spin dryer is big enough before you start. Twin tubs can usually handle a single or thin double. Automatics can do doubles, but not usually king-size; although wool blankets take up less room when wet, wet acrylics do not reduce in bulk. Hang outside if possible over two lines about 90 cm (3 ft) apart.

☐ **Pillows**

Down and feather pillows can be aired occasionally outside. Avoid washing unless absolutely necessary, as this removes oil from the feathers. But badly soiled pillows can be gently squeezed through a warm soapy solution, and rinsed well with three changes of water. Spin dry for two minutes if possible. Hang up by two corners and shake occasionally during drying. Or take to a professional cleaner.

Polyester pillows, e.g. Dacron, can be washed as above, but consult care label. They should not be dry-cleaned and should never be put in a tumble-dryer. Some pillows can be washed in a front-loading machine.

Latex pillows can usually be sponged clean, but if badly saturated the whole pillow can be washed, preferably still in its inner case as latex deteriorates on exposure to light. Use warm soapsuds, and do not twist or wring. Rinse well. Squeeze out as much moisture as possible into dry towel. Leave pillow in warm airing cupboard or in front of fan heater until dry.

THE KITCHEN & THE BATHROOM

For the sake of hygiene it is essential to keep the kitchen and bathroom scrupulously clean. Specific cleaning problems related to these areas of the home are dealt with in this chapter, from defrosting the fridge to cleaning ceramic bath tiles. For general advice refer to Chapter 2 Floors and Floor Coverings, page 13, and for maintaining walls, ceilings and woodwork, see Chapter 5 Other Household Surfaces, page 47.

THE KITCHEN

☐ Useful tips

● To reduce the problems caused by cooking fumes, an extractor fan will help to remove grease before it can settle on surfaces.

● Regularly wash down all work surfaces and chopping boards with a bowl of water to which a tablespoon of household bleach has been added or a solution of two teaspoons of Lifeguard disinfectant to 600 ml (1 pint) of water.

● Germs breed in cracks and crevices, so throw away chopping boards or chinaware, etc., that is cracked.

● Change kitchen hand-towels and tea towels often.

● Pour a little neat household bleach down your sink every day, and once a week pour a little down the outside drain.

● Clean out the vegetable container before refilling with a weak solution of household bleach and allow to dry thoroughly before putting back the food.

● Bread bins should be washed out once a week with a weak solution of household bleach and rinsed well. Never allow stale bread to accumulate. Allow the bin to dry thoroughly before putting bread back in.

● Defrost and clean the fridge and freezer regularly.

● Clean out food cupboards when necessary. First brush out any crumbs or spilt foods. Then wipe inside and outside with weak solution of household bleach, making sure you get into all the cracks and crevices. Leave doors open and allow to dry thoroughly before putting food back.

● Line pedal bins with newspaper or use a plastic bin liner. Strain liquids off refuse and wrap in newspaper before putting in bin. After emptying, wash out bin with solution of household disinfectant or bleach and allow to dry before re-lining. In hot weather, use disinfectant powder in outside dustbins. Keep lids on dustbins at all times.

☐ Washing-up

Relatively few people in Britain own a dish-washing machine. For most of us, it's still a sink-and-mop affair. We all have our own ways of tackling the dreaded chore, but do keep the following points in mind.

● A brush is usually more effective than a mop. A long-handled washing-up brush is useful for corners of pans etc., and a bottle brush comes in handy for inaccessible insides. A nylon scourer is good for cookware, and you will probably also need something stronger, such as a Brillo pad; rinse as little as possible because the soap inhibits rust.

● Dishcloths should be boiled or sterilized frequently in a solution of household bleach (following directions on bottle); and should be replaced as soon as they begin to wear out. Never use them to wipe the floor.

● Make sure you have somewhere convenient to leave dishes to drain; a wall-fixed plate rack is ideal, but make the fixing really firm, as this is heavy when loaded. If you are short of draining board space, a tea-towel spread out on an adjacent surface can take draining saucepans, etc., or put a plate rack on a tin or plastic tray.

● Do not throw everything into the sink during the cooking and dishing-up and table clearing stages. At some point it all has to be taken out again. Put dirty utensils in a spare washing up bowl, or on a tray or trolley.

● A rubber splash-guard on your tap will help cut down risk of chipping plates and glasses.

- Always wash glasses first. Glasses used for milk or alcohol should be rinsed in cold water before washing.
- If two glasses have stuck together put some cold water into the inner one, and then stand the outer one in a bowl of warm water. Leave a few moments, then ease apart.
- Don't leave items with wood, bone, china or plastic handles soaking in the bowl.
- Add a spoonful of mustard to your water to get rid of fish smells on silverware. Smells on knife blades from fish or onions can be rubbed with a little dry mustard on a damp cloth.

Pans: a general note   Always follow any manufacturer's instructions for 'conditioning' a new pan – this often involves a coating of cooking oil. In general, wash in hot water with a squeeze of washing-up liquid. It really does not matter if the outside of pans are less than pristine. Anyway, pans with a non-reflective external surface are supposed to cook better. Very greasy pans can be boiled up with a little detergent. Add a little vinegar to remove fishy smells. Fill burnt pans with cold water, add tablespoon of vinegar and boil for five minutes. Or turn pan upside down over another pan of boiling water, and steam off burnt deposits. Soak overnight. Or try soaking with biological detergent.

Non-stick pans   Soak burnt deposits for a few minutes. If necessary rub with nylon scourer – never a metal one. When badly stained, half fill with water, and add 1 tablespoon of bleach and 1 tablespoon of vinegar. Simmer for about 10 minutes in a well ventilated kitchen. Then wash and rinse, and re-oil.

Aluminium pans   They can be scoured with wire wool, but do not use copper pads or washing soda, which can set up harmful reactions. Aluminium discolours easily but the discoloration is not poisonous. You can prevent blackening when boiling an egg by adding 1 teaspoon of vinegar. To clean discoloured insides, simmer a solution of vinegar, or an acid fruit such as rhubarb; or fill with water, add 1 teaspoon of cream of tartar and bring to the boil and simmer for a few minutes. Food or fat left in pans can cause pitting.

Stainless steel pans   You can use a scourer such as a Brillo pad. Soak burnt deposits for as little as possible as pans may become pitted. Vinegar will remove blue stains caused by overheating, or use a stainless steel cleaner.

Cast iron pans   Always dry at once and, if uncoated, rub with cooking oil to prevent rust.

Copper saucepans   These are usually lined (commonly with tin) to prevent toxic reaction with food acids. Try and avoid scouring, which may damage linings, and similarly do not overheat – only a low light is necessary. Use copper cleaner on the outside from the Copper Shop or Prestige, or rub with cut lemon dipped in salt. Egg bowls are unlined, as the copper helps to make whites stiff and firmly textured when beating them for soufflés, meringues, sponge cakes and pavlovas. Similarly, copper preserving pans are traditionally unlead. You must scrub these utensils thoroughly before use (to remove poisonous deposits) with salt and cut lemons, until all discoloration has gone. Then wash in hot water and dry thoroughly before using.

Ceramic glass pans   Use only nylon scourers – most deposits should come off with soaking. A solution of household bleach will remove stains.

Enamel pans   Soak off burnt deposits. Use nylon, not metal, scourers. Use a solution of household bleach for stains or Chempro T.

Tinware (e.g. cake tins, baking trys and tins, ring moulds etc.) Usually made from mild steel coated with tin. Do not use abrasive cleaners, these can scratch the coating and cause the base metal to rust. Soak burnt food deposits in warm water and washing-up liquid. Badly discoloured tinware can be boiled up in a solution of washing soda (not for aluminium though). Soften rusty patches with a little oil or grease before scouring very gently. Dry thoroughly before storing; pop them into the oven while it is still warm, or leave on cooker plate-rack, or over radiator. New tinware can be greased with a butter or other fat wrapping paper and heated in a moderate oven for 15 minutes to give a virtually life-long protection against rust.

Cake and biscuit storage tins should be washed and dried thoroughly before putting away: allow to air on cooker rack, in cooling oven or over radiator, or give a brief blow with a hair dryer.

Vacuum flasks   Clean with a bottle brush; or fill with hot water containing a teaspoon of bicarbonate of soda, and leave to soak. Rinse and dry, then store open with stopper and cup removed. If flasks become stained or smell musty, fill with a cup of warm water mixed with a tablespoon of vinegar. Add pieces of eggshell, then swill round. Leave to stand, then swill mixture round again. Rinse well and allow to dry thoroughly. Stuff kitchen paper loosely in the top to stop dust getting in.

Kettles Remove fur with special de-scaling fluid from hardware shops, e.g. Oust, Ataka, Chempro or Scalefree. Follow directions carefully. Store with lid off. Special products are made for jug kettles: check directions carefully.

Wooden tableware (e.g. bread and cheese boards) Wipe clean after use, but do not wash unless absolutely necessary. Marks can be removed by rubbing with very fine steel wool moistened with a little olive oil. Apply olive oil when new and occasionally as necessary, blotting off excess with kitchen paper. Never leave woodware soaking in water (this particularly applies to wooden cutlery handles). Always wipe dry after washing and leave to air and dry completely after washing. Never dry near direct heat.

Cutlery Always wash as soon as possible. Many foods can cause staining or even pitting. Polish silver and stainless steel with appropriate branded cleaners. Do not place cutlery in dishwashers unless specifically recommended by manufacturer. Never leave cutlery with handles of a different material, i.e. bone, wood, china or plastic, soaking in water.

Stainless steel-bladed kitchen knives will not rust and will hold a sharp edge for some while. Carbon steel blades will rust, so always dry scrupulously after use, and sharpen regularly as they blunt more quickly. Rub blades clean with a Brillo pad.

China Try rubbing stained cups etc., with a damp cloth dipped in bicarbonate of soda, or soak overnight in hot washing soda solution, then rub cloth dipped in vinegar and salt. Or use proprietary stain removers such as Oust or Chempro T.

Plastic tableware Stains can be removed with denture cleaner or with stain remover Chempro T or bicarbonate of soda paste.

Teapots Clean silver and stainless steel teapots by soaking with hot water plus tablespoon of washing soda. Never use washing soda on chrome or aluminium. Aluminium – put 2 tablespoons of borax and add boiling water. Chromium – clean inside with cloth moistened with vinegar and dipped in salt. For china, see above. A teapot spout brush is handy, and a sugar lump will keep a stored teapot free from mustiness.

Glassware Always wash separately to avoid chipping. Rinse glasses used for milk or alcohol in cold water. Wash fine crystal and glass by hand; a soft old toothbrush will dislodge any dust trapped in patterns. Everyday tumblers can go in a dishwasher. Fill stained or cloudy glass

▶ *The Kitchen & the Bathroom*

with water plus 2 teaspoons of ammonia and leave overnight, rinse well. Soak hard water stains in distilled or rain-water. Very badly stained glass can be soaked in 1 cup of caustic soda to 2 litres (4 pints) of warm water, take care and rinse thoroughly. Polish up with impregnated silver wadding which also shifts stains. To clean a stained decanter, fill it half full with vinegar and cooking salt. Add half a cup of sand, if possible, or raw rice grains. Swill this mixture around the inside, you may have to repeat process several times. Alternatively, try vinegar and tea leaves which is good for lime deposits, or use Chempro T. Trickle a few drops of cooking oil or glycerine around a stuck stopper and leave overnight.

☐ **Plastic laminate surfaces**

These are used for work surfaces, tables, cabinet fronts, etc. Examples are Formica and Perstorp Warerite. Always wipe up spills as soon as possible as stains get worse if left. In particular beware of blackcurrant juice, hair dyes, paint strippers, etc., which may be impossible to remove if left. Both glossy and matt-finished laminates should be wiped down with warm water plus a few drops of washing-up liquid. Rinse well with clean water to avoid streaks. This is the only cleaning treatment recommended for glossy laminates.

Matt finished laminates (often used for kitchen work surfaces) may stain if liquids or food are left for any length of time. To remove stains, take half a cup of bicarbonate of soda and fill up with water. Apply this paste to the stain, cover with a piece of paper or polythene. Leave for couple of hours, then rinse off. Alternatively, try a mild solution of domestic bleach (1 part bleach to 5 parts water). Apply to stain for two minutes only, then rinse off thoroughly. (NB. prolonged contact with bleach can harm the surface – never use undiluted bleach.) Cream cleaners such as Jif will shift stains but you should only rub very lightly, as these are abrasives and could harm the surface. For obstinate food deposits, trickle a little water over them and leave to 'soak' for five minutes. The uneven surface of textured laminates can be very difficult to clean. Spilt liquids such as milk cannot be removed merely by wiping and will dry as an ugly stain. Use fine stiff-bristled brush, plus warm water with a few drops of washing-up liquid, then wash down with plenty of clean water.

☐ **Cookers**

Always make sure an electric cooker is switched off at the main cooker control panel before cleaning. Read carefully any manufacturer's directions which relate to cleaning – follow their advice.

To cut cleaning problems, always try and wipe down hob after each time of use. Wipe up spills immediately but do be careful not to touch any parts which are still very hot.

For stubborn marks, use a little cream cleaner of the type approved by the VEDC (Vitreous Enamel Development Council – look for their label on the cleaner pack – see symbol diagram below). Avoid harsh scouring pads or powders which can scratch enamels. If possible soak burnt-on stains under a little water, or wet the stain and leave for a few minutes before tackling it. Hardened sugar deposits, caused for example by jam boiling over, can be softened with a solution of 2 tablespoons washing soda to 0.5 litre (1 pint) of boiling water. Use an old toothbrush for fiddly knobs. Many knobs can be removed for cleaning (check manufacturer's instructions).

| | **VITREOUS ENAMEL DEVELOPMENT COUNCIL** | **Tested and recommended for use on vitreous enamel** |

This symbol means a cleaner has been approved for use on enamel surfaces.

You can lift off removable parts and soak in sink and then wash with hot water and washing-up liquid solution. Rinse, dry well and replace. Glass oven doors can usually be removed for cleaning at the sink. Use only nylon scouring pads and paste cleaners as steel wool could scratch the glass. Do not use aerosol oven cleaners on glass doors.

Always try and clean your oven while it is still warm but not hot. You can remove shelves and other movable parts and soak/wash with hot water and detergent solution. On very dirty ovens you can use a proprietary oven cleaner but follow manufacturer's instructions to the letter. Do not clean self-clean oven linings, otherwise you will spoil the special surface (refer to maker's instructions).

□ **Sinks**

Boiling water and washing soda poured down waste pipes weekly will keep pipe clear from grease. Never pour hot fat down the sink: it can set solid in the pipe.

Enamel and porcelain   Use a cream cleaner, e.g. Jif. Diluted household bleach can be used on obstinate marks (put in plug and allow solution to stand). Or try Liftoff, but follow directions carefully. Rub brown iron stains with a paste of cream of tartar and hydrogen peroxide, scrubbed well in and then rinsed away. A plastic washing-up bowl will protect from chipping, and use a plastic mat or plate rack on enamel draining boards.

Stainless steel   For daily cleaning use washing-up liquid or a cream cleaner, e.g. Jif. Try and avoid spilling neat bleach, salt or undissolved detergent powders on sink or draining board which can cause pitting. Silver-cleaning solutions can cause permanent stains, and hot splashes of fat may cause rainbow marks. To shift very obstinate or old stains, use stainless steel cleaner such as Polaris or Prestige.

THE BATHROOM

Multi-purpose cream cleaners have been developed for the bathroom, e.g. Impact and Mr Muscle. They come in trigger packs, and will help clear clinging lime deposits.

☐ Baths

Always follow any manufacturer's care notes provided with a new bath. Regular cleaning prevents stains, and it is best done when the bath is still warm. To avoid hard water stains, finish off with a rinse, and then rub dry with soft cloth. A shower attachment is useful.

Bath salts help soften the water and prevent scum. But make sure they are well-dissolved, as their gritty texture can cause scratching. Add them to the water under the taps while the bath is running. A Minky bathroom cloth cleans one side and dries on the other.

Never fill any type of bath with photo solutions and take great care when washing large sharp-edged items in the bath such as venetian blinds.

Enamelled baths   Use cleaners, as recommended by the Vitreous Enamel Development Council (look for mark on pack). Avoid harsh scouring powders. Special stain removers are available from hardware shops for use on badly-stained old enamelled baths. Try them on a corner of the bath first, and follow directions carefully. Or try a paste of tartar and hydrogen peroxide applied with great care to stains with a nylon brush, scrubbed vigorously and then rinsed off. Cut lemons with cooking salt, or white vinegar, will sometimes remove brown iron stains – repeat several times, rinsing after each application. Green copper stains will sometimes respond to a solution of soapy water and a little ammonia, or try lemon juice or vinegar. Scrub and rinse.

For very obstinate stains on enamelled baths, and really only when all else fails, apply a solution of 1 part oxalic acid crystals to 20 parts of water, but proceed with caution, wearing rubber gloves, as this is very poisonous. Use a china basin and wooden spoon and apply to stain with cotton mop. As soon as stain has shifted, neutralize with a solution of washing soda and rinse well. Neutralize any remaining solution of oxalic acid with washing soda crystals and pour down the lavatory; flush well. Or use Ataka. But for all methods test a small area with cotton wool first and wear rubber gloves.

Plastic baths   In general use only a little washing-up liquid on a cloth dampened with warm water. In hard water areas, use a cream cleaner (e.g. Jif, Gumption) from time to time. Small scratches and dulled patches can be removed with metal polish; apply to a dry surface, then rinse well. For deeper scratches, rub with fine wire wool before applying metal polish. Certain substances harm plastic baths: beware of paint strippers and some paints, nail varnish and varnish removers.

☐ **Lavatories**

Keep your loo scrupulously clean; it will look better, smell sweeter and most important of all, will prevent germs spreading around the home. Use a weak solution of household bleach to wash over seat, outside of bowl, cover, cistern and cistern handle. Use a cloth kept solely for that purpose. Clean round bowl with lavatory brush, and then rinse brush well or it may deteriorate. Don't forget to clean the area behind the loo with disinfectant solution, and also the surrounding wall and floor. Once a week, clean bowl more thoroughly with lavatory cleaner, e.g. Harpic powder which will dissolve the limescale, or leave undiluted bleach in bowl overnight. *But never mix bleach and lavatory cleaner together*, the resulting fumes are highly toxic – even lethal.

Thick liquids are available to remove limescale and kill germs, e.g. Harpic Jet Power. Other detergent liquids have a pleasant fragrance for daily use. Cistern and bowl blocks can be installed to clean the bowl every time it is flushed.

☐ Basins and bidets

Clean as for baths, but pay special attention to overflows, which can harbour black slime and matted hairs. Clean with an old toothbrush, bottle brush or pipe cleaner using neat household disinfectant or household bleach.

☐ Taps

Clean regularly to avoid dirt building up. An old toothbrush is useful for the area around the taps. Kleeneze make a special 'U'-shaped brush. Wipe chrome-plated taps with a cloth wrung out in warm water and detergent; if very dirty use a little cream bath cleaner. To restore dulled old chrome finishes, buy a special chrome cleaner from a car accessory shop. Gold-plated taps should be cleaned with a barely damp cloth with minimum rubbing.

☐ Showers

From time to time unscrew shower head, rinse out hard water scale: you can buy special cleaners for this, e.g. Oust. Mould on the bottom of a shower curtain should be wiped over with a mild solution of domestic bleach. Rub hard water deposits (a white clinging film) with vinegar and then rinse well with clean water.

☐ Ceramic tiles

These can be washed with a sudsy solution of washing-up liquid and a mild cream cleanser for stubborn marks, but don't use harsh liquids and brushes which might spoil the glaze. Add a few drops of disinfectant to soapy water for areas adjacent to the lavatory. Near a shower or bath, hard water may leave lime deposits which can be shifted with white vinegar applied neat and left for ten minutes. Rinse, dry, and polish with a dry cloth or try Mr Muscle Ceramic Tile Restorer. Grouting between tiles can be cleaned with an old toothbrush and a solution of domestic bleach. But very badly discoloured grouting is best raked out and re-done.

☐ Face flannels and sponges

Boil regularly in water with few drops of vinegar to get rid of slime. Soak slimy sponges in salt and cold water. Always squeeze out flannels and sponges and leave to dry after use; hang flannels up.

·5·

OTHER HOUSEHOLD SURFACES

While it may not be necessary to tackle the cleaning tasks described in this chapter every week, or even every month, it is important for the maintenance of your home and the possessions in it, that you do these jobs as often as is necessary.

WALLS

☐ Painted walls

Take down pictures, push furniture into middle of room (get help if necessary) and cover, turn back or protect floorings . . . however careful you know you'll be! Take down curtains or tie back. If the ceiling is dirty too, it is a good idea to wash this before the walls (see page 48). First brush down with soft brush (or duster tied over broom head) to remove as much loose dirt as possible; better still, use vacuum cleaner with soft brush attachment (make sure it is clean to start with). Then wash, using sponge or cloth or sponge floor mop well wrung out in bucket of warm water plus squeeze of washing-up liquid. Do not use soap powders: they contain 'fluorescers' which brighten your clothes but may change colour of paints.

Work from skirting upwards; this is because water runs can 'set' dirt and make it very difficult to remove. Treat very dirty patches with a little neat washing-up liquid or cleaning powder. Then wipe over with sponge or cloth wrung out in clean water, have a second bucket or bowl with clear, warm rinsing water handy, working this time from top to bottom. Work in strips about 90 cm (3 ft) wide, completing whole wash-and-wipe operation before moving on to fresh section. But try and finish a whole wall in one go, otherwise you may get a line where the cleaning stopped. Before washing round switches or power points, turn off electricity at the mains.

☐ **Wallpapered walls**

Washable wallpaper is in fact *only* spongeable. Use a cloth or sponge damped in a bucket of warm water plus a squeeze of washing-up liquid, working from the bottom up. Rinse with cloth well wrung-out in clear water (have two buckets readily available). Do not rub or overwet. Do not use white spirit or other solvents which may damage the wallpaper finish.

Non-washable wallpaper Try pieces of bread to remove dirty marks. Alternatively, rub gently with a soft pencil rubber. Grease marks can be dabbed cautiously with a clean pad moistened with a branded stain-removal solvent or use an aerosol stain remover (but try these on an out-of-sight area first); or marks may respond to a warm iron placed over a piece of blotting paper.

Vinyl wallcoverings can be washed with washing-up liquid (see washable wallpaper, above), depending how dirty the wall is. Do not overwet. Clean a small area at a time, and wipe off as you go with warm water and a clean cloth. Work upwards from floor level and avoid rubbing across the joints. Treat stains with a very small amount of white spirit, or rub lightly with scouring powder (e.g. Ajax) and a cloth, then wipe off with clean cloth wrung out in warm water, but do not use these treatments on vinyls with metallic colours. Where vinyl coverings have worked loose at the joints, you can re-stick with Copydex.

Fabric and speciality wallcoverings (such as hessians and grasscloths) In general simply dust down, if possible using a vacuum cleaner with soft brush. Marks, stains, etc., may respond to a treatment with an aerosol stain-removal solvent (dry cleaner) but always try out on an out-of-sight area first (e.g. where wallcovering is covered by a piece of furniture). Many of these coverings may shrink or lose their colour if wetted with water, or cleaned with a solvent.

CEILINGS

☐ **Painted celings**

Enclose any light fittings in large plastic bags (carriers do fine) stuck up with masking tape. Cover floor and furniture with plastic sheeting. Wash and rinse as for painted walls (page 47).

□ **Papered ceilings**

Before beginning work, prepare the ceiling and room as above. Wash and rinse as for papered walls (page 48).

□ **Polystyrene ceiling tiles**

They can be dusted by attaching a duster or soft cloth to the head of a broom, or with a vacuum cleaner and soft brush attachment. If they need washing, use a solution of detergent and warm water then rinse. Do not press tiles as they will dent. You can give these a coat of emulsion (i.e. water-based) paint, preferably fire-resistant (e.g. Timonex). Never use an oil-based paint or white spirit because this increases the fire risk.

□ **Lampshades**

When cleaning, switch off pendants, or remove plug from socket for table lamps. Take off shade.

Washable fabric lampshades Remove any coloured trimmings which might run. The whole shade may be swished through a bowl of warm soapy water; rinse in clear lukewarm water and dry away from heat. Some elasticated shades will slip off the frame for washing.

Non-washable fabrics or delicate shades Use professional dry-cleaner. Or simply dust down well, removing any marks from dirt or grease with a cloth moistened with branded grease-removal solvent. Or you can try dipping a pad of clean cotton wool into oatmeal; run this over the shade. Leave for ten minutes and then rub off lightly, using a clean pad of cloth.

Parchment lampshades Add 1 teaspoon of soap flakes to 1 teaspoon of warm water. Stir, then add 2 teaspoons of methylated spirit (flammable) and stir once more. Sponge this solution on to shade with clean, soft cloth. Wipe off lather. Now rub shade over with cloth dipped in methylated spirit. Allow to dry. Polish with soft dry cloth. To renew sheen, wipe with cloth moistened with olive oil.

Plastic lampshades Wash with warm water and detergent solution. Allow a weak water and detergent solution to dry on shade to cut down dirt attraction.

Chandeliers These can be cleaned in minutes with Hagarty's spray-on Chandelier Cleaner, which loosens the dirt and causes it to drop off.

▶ *Other Household Surfaces*

PAINTED WOODWORK

Dust regularly. Remove marks with a damp cloth plus washing-up liquid solution, then rinse off; or use cream cleaner, or aerosol or trigger general purpose cleaner but avoid solutions containing ammonia, which can attack the paint film. You can use a little white spirit on black marks. When very dirty, wash down using methods described for painted walls (page 47). You can use an old soft toothbrush to shift grime in mouldings. White gloss paint (oil-based paint) that has yellowed cannot be brightened by cleaning. The yellowing is in the paint itself and re-painting is the only effectively solution.

WINDOWS

☐ **Window panes**

Choose a warm dull day for cleaning if possible. Various branded cleaners are available in bottles, aerosols or trigger packs but can be expensive. Impregnated cloths are made specially for cleaning windows, e.g. Minky. A longer-term investment is a rubber squeegee, which leaves windows smear-free, and can fit on to a broom handle for out-of-reach panes. Telescopic versions are available to reach upper floors (Kleeneze). Use a bucket of warm water, plus a few drops of ammonia. Start at the top left edge of the window and draw the squeegee across. Return to the left edge, overlapping the first slightly and repeat. Continue in this way. Newspaper is good for finishing off, as newsprint has a solvent action and the paper absorbs final traces of moisture. Stubborn fly marks can be removed with methylated spirit (flammable).

☐ **Curtains**

Clean or wash regularly to stop sunlight, dirt, etc., spoiling the fabric. Lined, interlined or large heavy curtains are best dry-cleaned. Also dry-clean if shrinking would be disastrous or if curtains have Milium insulating linings.

When washing, remove hooks, store carefully. You can use a small dab of nail varnish to indicate hook positions. Pull out gathers so that heading is flat; for this reason never cut string in curtain tape, but wind it neatly round a patent cord-tidy or tuck it behind tape. Shake or brush curtains to remove loose dirt. Soak curtains for 10 minutes in cold water with a little liquid detergent (e.g. Stergene). Rinse, remove as much water as possible and then wash by hand or gentlest machine programme according to fabric. Be gentle; fabric may have been weakened by exposure to sun, etc., and be vulnerable when wet. Glass fibre curtains should be hand washed in the bath to avoid cracking. Drip dry without folding.

☐ Net curtains

These should be washed frequently, separately from natural fibres, and rinsed thoroughly (detergent scum can dull brightness). Soak first in cold water with detergent solution (e.g. Stergene) then hand wash in hand-hot water. You can soak, wash, and rinse with nets folded to reduce wrinkles. For machines, wash on synthetics cycle, maximum temperature 50°C but cooler temperatures can be used to reduce creasing, if nets are not too dirty. Never boil. Drip-drying will minimize creasing. Never wring nets – and only spin dry for a very short time. If you wish to tumble dry, set on lowest temperature, and allow to tumble with heat off until nets have cooled to minimize creasing. Hang nets immediately – a warm iron can be used first if necessary. Special solutions are available for brightening dulled net curtains. (Dylon Simply White or Kleeneze Net Curtain Whitener.)

☐ Blinds

Fabric roller blinds can usually be wiped clean with a damp cloth at the window if lightly soiled, but take down if fairly dirty and spread out on floor protected with old sheet, newspaper etc. But never use cleaning solvents; these will dissolve the protective finish. Traditional holland blinds can only be dusted down; a vacuum cleaner with soft brush attachment may be used.

Venetian blinds   Apart from the top section which may rust, these can be soaked in a bath in a weak solution of detergent and then rinsed in clean water. Take care not to scratch bath enamel. To clean blinds without taking them down, you can use one of the special gadgets available that cleans several slats at the same time. (Kleeneze Venetian Blind Duster.) Or simply put on old fabric gloves and use your fingers to wipe the slats clean.

FIREPLACES

For light soiling on brickwork brush with soft brush and then scrub with hard brush and clean warm water. If soiling persists, try washing down with neat vinegar, followed by thorough rinsing. Never use soap or detergents, which may leave deposits that cannot be removed. Buy a proprietary soot remover from a builders' merchant or fireplace specialist and apply to the front of the bricks. Or make up a solution of 1 part spirits of salts to 6 parts water and apply this to the brick surfaces only, not the pointing in between. Wash down quickly and thoroughly with plenty of warm water. Take care to wear thick rubber gloves, and goggles to protect your eyes, because this is a strong corrosive, with poisonous fumes. Maintain a good level of ventilation and don't lean over your work. Burn marks on the bricks can be wiped over with vinegar and then rinsed off with clear, warm water.

For light soiling on stone scrub with clear warm water and then mop with a sponge to soak up water, dirt and grit. You can add a few drops of washing-up liquid to the water, then rinse well, but don't use soap, soap powders, scouring powders or heavy-duty cleaning liquids which may affect the colouring of the stone. A stronger treatment is to scrub with a strong solution of domestic bleach, taking care to protect surrounding area, and rinsing well.

For ceramic tiles see page 46. Don't treat tiles while still hot or the glaze could crack or the tiles split. A few drops of furniture cream can be included in the cleaning process.

   Stainless steel trims can be polished with a cleaner/polisher such as Polaris or Prestige.

For treatment of marble see page 57.

PICTURE GLASS AND MIRRORS

Clean picture glass and mirrors as for window panes, see page 50. Dried hair spray can be removed from mirrors with methylated spirit (but do be careful as this is highly flammable). Use the Magic Touch anti-mist glove to keep glass, mirrors and windscreens from misting up.

BOOKS

Try to dust books regularly. Always blow away dust or wipe top first with soft cloth before opening pages. A vacuum cleaner soft brush attachment is handy for the tops of books in bookcases. The jackets of leather-bound books can be wiped with a solution of warm water, soap flakes and a little glycerine, then apply special hide food, Hidelife, made by Bridge of Weir.

METALS

In general metals tarnish, rust or corrode through reaction with air, aggravated by damp.

☐ Aluminium

Anodized aluminium can be wiped clean with a damp cloth and polished off with a dry soft cloth; do not use abrasives. For aluminium pans etc., see page 39.

☐ Brass

Moisture in the air can cause brass to first tarnish and finally to corrode. Wash tarnished brass in hot soapy water with a cupful of ammonia and dry. Then, polish with Brasso to remove tarnish and 'heal' scratches (the polish actually makes the metal flow into the scratch marks). Lemon dipped in salt removes mild corrosion, as does salt and vinegar. For severe corrosion, dab on spirits of salts (hydrochloric acid) using a rag tied to a stick. This acid is very poisonous and corrosive so wear gloves and avoid splashing skin or eyes. Rinse well. Alternatively, try soaking overnight in a handful of washing soda to a bowl of hot water; then rinse, dry and polish.

Treat lacquered brass with a damaged finish with acetone to remove the lacquer. Then polish and re-spray with lacquer if you wish.

Items not regularly handled can be given a thin coating of Vaseline, olive oil, or furniture cream to prevent tarnish. Brass curtain rings and hooks can be soaked in boiling water plus a capful of ammonia to remove tarnish.

Special cleaners and lacquer removers are available from Knobs and Knockers, or you can buy Magic Touch polishing mitts.

☐ Bronze

Generally bronze needs only dusting and polishing with a dry cloth. A very little oil polished off with a dry cloth will give an attractive sheen and guard against corrosion. Very dirty articles can be washed in a hot detergent solution or rubbed over with turpentine or paraffin (caution: both are flammable). Rinse and dry thoroughly. Wendol is a multimetal polish suitable for bronze, aluminium, chrome, stainless steel, pewter, nickel, brass and copper. Store bronze cutlery carefully as the metal is fairly soft. Do not put in dishwasher and use metal polish if necessary.

☐ **Chrome**

Chrome used inside a home should only need wiping over with a cloth rung out in warm water. Rinse and dry thoroughly. Avoid abrasives or neat bleach. Try Wendol on very greasy areas; on grimy chrome, use a dry cloth with a little bicarbonate of soda. For discoloration and pitting, use a chrome cleaner available from car accessory shops.

☐ **Copper**

Tarnish should respond to a rub with a piece of lemon dipped in salt and vinegar. Rub hard and rinse well with hot soapy water. Dry and burnish to a shine. Or use a proprietary copper cleaner, such as Prestige Copper Cleaner or Hagerty Copper Wash or a metal cleaner, e.g. Brasso. Special cleaners are available from the Copper Shop.

Copper saucepans are usually lined (e.g. with tin) and should be re-lined when necessary. When unlined copper comes into contact with acid foods (e.g. fruits) it develops a poisonous substance called verdigris. Use wood or plastic utensils to preserve linings.

☐ **Gold**

Gold items can be washed in a warm detergent solution plus a capful of ammonia, rinsed and polished with a soft dry cloth. Hagerty Jewel Clean is especially good for gold and platinum.

☐ **Iron and steel**

With the exception of stainless steel both these metals will rust if left exposed to the air and unprotected by grease or 'primer' plus paint. Remember that rust is not only ugly but also corrosive, i.e. it will 'eat' through metal in time. Rust removers are available from hardware shops and car accessory shops – follow directions carefully as some contain potentially dangerous chemicals. Then grease (or prime plus paint) the bare clean metal. 'Berlin Black' is a special paint for ironwork with a matt black finish. Heatproof Stove Black is also available (Rustins). You can revive the black finish on ironwork with Zebrite black metal polish – rub on with a soft cloth.

☐ **Pewter**

Clean pewter regularly to prevent tarnish. Wash in warm soapy water and dry with a soft cloth. You can use methylated spirit (inflammable) to restore the sheen, or buy a metal polish such as Wendol, but do not use this on mirror-finish pewter, which can be cleaned with Long Term Silver Foam. Do not wash in dishwashers.

☐ **Silver**

Sulphur and moisture in the air causes brown then black tarnish on silver which eventually corrodes the metal and can usually be polished off, although by doing so, you are removing a minute part of the surface of silver. Egg, fish, green vegetables, fruit juices, sugar, mustard, salt and vinegar stain all silverware, so always rinse cutlery immediately after use. Soak off mustard in cold water. Perfumes and toiletwater may also be harmful. Do not leave decayed fruit in silver bowls or wilting flowers in vases – change water frequently. Remove all candlewax with hot water or white spirit – do not scrape. Never put silver in hot oven. Stained tea and coffee pots can be soaked for one hour in a bowl of hot water with a tablespoon of washing soda dissolved in it. Open fires encourage tarnish.

There are many proprietary cleaners available for silver, including cloths and polishes which retard tarnish, polishing mitts by Magic Touch and gloves and rinse-off foams for intricate pieces. Polish off with chamois leather, which should be used until completely clogged. Then wash 'chammy' in hot water with household bar soap (e.g. Sunlight), rinse and repeat until clean. Rub more soap into leather and leave to dry without rinsing. Rub leather between hands or beat against wooden table until soft. Silver Dip (by Goddards or Hagerty) is useful for cutlery, but do not soak joint between knife handle and blade. And never use on hollow items, or items with detailed decoration or with cavities; trapped dip solution can corrode indefinitely. Always rinse thoroughly after use in cold then hot water and dry with clean cloth.

Scratches over silver can be removed by applying jewellers' rouge (available from jewellers) mixed with methylated spirit. Apply with a finger. Solutions are now available for replating worn silver such as 'The Silver Solution' by Sheffio and 'Silver Plating Formula' by Anthony Green.

Keep silver or silver plate in a box or bag, or drawer with soft lining to avoid scratches; if silver is not in regular use wrap in polythene bags, to exclude air and prevent tarnishing. Or use specially-shaped tarnishretardent Hagerty or Magic Touch cloth bags. A Silver Keeper (Hagerty) will release a harmless vapour to prevent tarnish in a drawer or box. Do not wrap in newspaper (printer's ink contains tarnish-forming sulphur), and do not secure bundles with rubber bands, which can corrode through several layers of paper.

☐ Stainless steel

Prolonged contact with water can cause pitting, so do not leave pans or cutlery soaking longer than necessary. Neat bleach, salt or undissolved detergent can also cause pitting. Silver-dipping cleaners will permanently stain stainless steel cutlery and sinks. Use Prestige cleaner specially formulated for stainless steel.

PRECIOUS MATERIALS

☐ Ebony

Do not wash. Dust regularly and occasionally apply a little furniture cream.

☐ Ivory

Dust with a soft brush or cloth and expose to sunlight for a bleaching effect (but not strong sun through glass). Do not put in water – ivory is semi-porous. Wash knives with ivory handles quickly in lukewarm water avoiding soaking handle. You can clean ivory with toothpaste applied with a cloth and polished off. Stains may respond to methylated or surgical spirit (caution flammable) but do not give this treatment to valuable antiques. When clean, coat ivory with almond oil (from a chemist) and leave 24 hours to soak in.

☐ Jewelry

All jewelry pieces of any value should be professionally and regularly cleaned and at the same time checked for necessary small repairs. Some jewelry should never be washed but only polished with soft cloth or brush: this includes pearls, marcasite, and porous stones such as opal and turquoise. Hard stones however (amethysts, diamonds, rubies and sapphires) can be washed quickly (do not soak) in warm water plus a few drops of washing-up liquid using a soft old toothbrush. For safety's sake use a small bowl or you could lose a precious ring down the drain! Rinse well and dry. Goddard's Jewellery Care is a liquid especially for cleaning fine jewelry. Hagerty make Pearl Clean and a Jewelry Cloth. Always store jewelry items separately to avoid scratching.

□ **Marble**

Mop up spills immediately – marble stains easily. You can use warm soapy water to sponge or scrub white marble adding a few drops of ammonia if staining is heavy. But test small area before using this treatment on coloured marble. Rinse and polish with dry white cloth. Hydrogen peroxide plus a few drops of ammonia may be effective for shifting some stains – leave for a few minutes before removing and repeat if necessary. Alternatively try a branded stain remover. Marble can be polished with a white silicone or wax furniture polish. Antiquax make a marble wax. Special cleaners and restorers are made by A. Bell who also make a Touch Up pack for chipped edges.

□ **Mother-of-pearl**

Take great care of this porous material which will easily stain. Do not soak cutlery handles. Try a little furniture cream on stains; rub gently.

□ **Onyx**

This is porous so always wipe up spills on table tops immediately. You can protect the surface with a good wax polish. Dust regularly and wipe over with barely damp cloth. Light marks may respond to methylated spirit.

► *Other Household Surfaces*

·6·

WASHING, DRYING & IRONING

BEFORE WASHING

☐ Look for the label

Most fabrics for clothes and furnishings look lovely when they are new. It is heart-breaking if they no longer look so good when washed and/or ironed, or dry-cleaned. A little attention to the correct methods will pay off.

Always look for the care label and read the instructions printed on it carefully.

Manufacturers are now compelled by law to label fabrics and garments with the name of fibre from which they are made. Unfortunately, they are not compelled to sew in or even attach washing or cleaning instructions, though this practice is now common among reputable manufacturers and retailers. On clothes, if you cannot find the label in the obvious place at the back of the neck or waist, try the side seams. Some people find labels irritating and cut them out; if you do this, slip the cut-off label into an envelope itself labelled with the name of the garment and keep somewhere safe for future reference. (Actually, it's not a bad idea, as many labels become unreadable after a few washes.) Keep carefully in a similar fashion any swing tickets or care leaflets. Some furnishing fabrics have care symbols printed on the selvedge.

☐ **Understanding the label**

Fabric labelling was pioneered in Britain by the Home Laundering Consultative Council (HLCC, founded in 1961) who helped to formulate the International Textile Care Labelling Code (ITCLC) introduced to Britain in 1974 and based on the symbols below.

Many labels spell out the information in words as well as symbols if you take the trouble to look. But Continental labels will be symbols only.

There are five main symbols to remember:

The washtub tells you how to wash.

The triangle tells you about bleaching.

The iron tells you about ironing.

The circle tells you about dry-cleaning.

The square tells you about drying.

▲ *Washing, Drying & Ironing*

Before 1987 British washtub symbols contained numbers above and below a central line. The number above referred to the correct washing 'programme' (governing the degree and length of agitation and length of spin speed) and the number below referred to the maximum temperature safe for washing the labelled article.

Now, however, British washtub symbols have been simplified to bring them into line with Continental practice. Wash programme numbers have been abolished and washtub symbols now only contain the maximum temperature at which the fabric can be washed without harm. A bar under the tub indicates whether an article should receive a minimum, medium or maximum wash, with reference to washing times and agitation levels. If there is no bar under the washtub, you can use the normal full and heaviest action of your machine. But if there is a bar under the washtub symbol you should reduce the action of your machine to medium. And a broken bar under the washtub means that the action of your machine should be reduced to its minimum.

The fabric care guide on page 61 explains how the new washtub symbols dovetail with the old. You will find this chart printed on washing powder packs.

The washtub symbol can contain a hand, which means 'hand-wash only'.

If any symbol is crossed through with a large X, this means emphatically 'do not'. So the bleach triangle crossed through means 'do not bleach'. The circle crossed through means 'do not dry-clean' and the iron crossed through means 'do not iron'.

☐ **Articles without labels**

If no washing intructions are given on care labels or swing tickets, look for the fibre label, which should be provided *by law*. You will find guidance on how to wash different fibres in the fabric care guide opposite. Otherwise wash in the mildest possible way. Do not soak. Hand-wash quickly and carefully or use the coolest, gentlest machine programme. Rinse thoroughly, roll in a towel to remove excess moisture and dry carefully (dry flat if colour may run or for heavy garments). If washability is in doubt, seek advice of a good cleaner.

☐ **Pack labelling**

To make choosing washing products easier, the Consumers' Association came to an agreement at the end of 1986 with the leading detergent manufacturers that certain information would from then on appear on all packs. It was agreed that packs should state whether the product contained enzymes, perfume, bleach and whiteners. The presence or absence of enzymes is likely to be described as 'biological' or 'non-biological' respectively. The pack should also tell you whether the product is low-sudsing and therefore suited for automatic front-loading machines (usually indicated by the single word 'automatic'). The pack should also state whether or not the product contains soap, as this can harm garments or furnishings with a flame-proof finish. This information won't appear in the same place on all packs and you may have to hunt around for it.

FABRIC CARE GUIDE

Textile/ Machine code Old | New	Machine	Handwash	Examples of Application
1/95°C 9/95° ⎍95	MAXIMUM wash in Cotton cycle.	Hand hot (50°C) or boil. Spin or wring.	White Cotton and Linen articles without special finishes.
2/60° 3/60° ⎍60	MAXIMUM wash in Cotton cycle.	Hand hot (50°C). Spin or wring.	Cotton, Linen or Viscose articles without special finishes where colours are fast at 60°C.
4/50° ⎍50	MEDIUM wash in Synthetics cycle.	Hand hot. Cold rinse, short spin, or damp dry.	Polyester/Cotton mixtures, nylon, polyester; cotton and viscose articles with special finishes. Cotton/Acrylic mixtures.
5/40° ⎍40	MAXIMUM wash in Cotton cycle.	Warm. Spin or wring.	Cotton, Linen or Viscose where colours are fast at 40°C but not at 60°C.
6/40° ⎍40	MEDIUM wash in Synthetics cycle.	Warm. Cold rinse, short spin do not hand wring.	Acrylics, Acetate and Triacetate; including mixtures with wool; polyester/wool blends.
7/40° ⎍40	MINIMUM wash in wool cycle.	Warm. Do not rub. Spin. Do not hand wring.	Wool, Wool mixed with other fibres; Silk.
8/30°	Articles labelled ⎍8/30° or ⎍30° should be washed in the appropriate MEDIUM or MINIMUM cycle or handwash.		The terms 'Minimum, Medium and Maximum Wash' refer to the washing time and agitation required. Follow the manufacturer's instructions.

⎍hand	Hand wash only (see garment label).	**Mixed Load Washing Advice** Select lowest wash temperature indicated on the labels. Where load contains labels with ⎍ and ⎍ symbols use the MEDIUM wash cycle at your selected temperature. Where ⎍40 appears always use the MINIMUM wash cycle.
⊠	Do not machine or handwash.	

WASHING BY MACHINE

A washing machine is now owned by 85 per cent of all UK households. Sixty per cent of households have front-loading automatics, whilst the remaining 25 per cent are single or twin-tub machines.

Always keep your machine instruction book handy. It is difficult to take in all the information in one go so re-read it from time to time. Be careful to use the specified amounts of powder; measure them as directed on the pack. Too little powder means half-dirty clothes; too much and it will not be rinsed properly. Automatics literally cannot get clothes clean unless you use the special low-lather powders sold for these machines. The washing programme is very important (see chart page 61). Washed for too long at too high temperatures, white fabrics may yellow, dyes can fade or stain other clothes, fibres can become distorted and fabrics can stretch, shrink or become permanently creased. Remove clothes from machine (or dryer) as soon as possible after washing is finished – this cuts down on creasing, particularly for synthetics.

☐ **In preparation for a machine wash**

1 Mend small tears or holes as these can get bigger in the wash. Sew on any loose buttons – they could get lost and/or damage the machine.

2 Empty pockets: coloured paper (e.g. train or bus tickets, a book of matches, or money) can stain; tissues can break up into a white fluff all over the rest of the wash and could block the machine. (Take disintegrated notes to the bank, and try to claim a refund.)

3 Brush off any loose dirt (patches of mud, etc.), pay particular attention to trouser turn-ups.

4 Close zips and fasteners: they may be damaged or cause damage if left open.

5 Tie tapes, apron strings, etc., in a loose bow, and button long sleeves to shirt or blouse front.

6 Treat heavily soiled areas with household bar soap, *not* a few grains of dampened detergent, which will be too strongly concentrated and could make colours go patchy. Examine stains and treat if necessary. Scrubbing will weaken fabrics: if you must scrub, do it from the back, to push dirt out the way it came in. Pre-wash aerosols are very effective.

7 Sort clothes into groups. Those with old washtub labels can be sorted according to the number on the label. Sort new washtub labels according to the temperature and degree of agitation indicated (see chart).

8 Put delicate items in an old pillow-case or in a washing machine net, also tights to stop them tying themselves in knots.

☐ **Mixed loads**

Ideally each fabric group should be washed on its own, but inevitably you will want to make up mixed loads. The general rule when mixing is always to choose the washing action and maximum temperature given for the least robust fabric in the group.

For garments with old washtub symbols you can mix codes 1 to 4, but always select the mildest programme (see chart). For example, fabrics from codes 1 and 2 should be washed as for code 2. Fabrics from codes 3 and 4 should be washed as for 4.

Do not mix articles from codes 5 to 8 or any white synthetics. They must always be washed on their own programmes. In particular, white nylons and white polyester/cottons should always be washed on their own, as they will pick up colours from the rest of the wash and become discoloured. *Where colours have run* during washing and become discoloured new products claim to restore them to their original colours. For example Colour Run and Run Away.

For garments with new washtub symbols, remember that the bottom bar under the washtub means take care when washing and use a reduced action on your machine. You can mix items with labels without a bar provided you wash at the lowest temperature shown in the tubs on the labels. You can mix items with labels with and without a bar, provided that, again, you wash at the lowest temperature shown and that you also reduce the washing action to a medium cycle. But never mix items with a broken bottom bar with other items: they must only be washed on the wool cycle with minimum agitation, at a maximum temperature of 40°C.

▲ *Washing, Drying & Ironing*

☐ Overloading

Overloading your machine means your clothes won't come out as clean as they might and your machine may be damaged. So check your instruction manual to find out the weight of maximum loads.

Here is a table showing the weight of some typical items in the household wash:

Clothes		Weight	
Blouse	Cotton	150 g	5 oz
	Other	100 g	$3\frac{1}{2}$ oz
Dress	Cotton	500 g	1 lb 2 oz
	Other	350 g	12 oz
Jeans		700 g	1 lb 8 oz
10 nappies		1000 g	2 lb 3 oz
Shirt	Cotton	300 g	$10\frac{1}{2}$ oz
	Other	200 g	7 oz
Tee-shirt		125 g	$4\frac{1}{2}$ oz
Household items			
Duvet cover (double)	Cotton	1500 g	3 lb 5 oz
	Other	1000 g	2 lb 3 oz
Large tablecloth	Cotton	700 g	1 lb 8 oz
Small tablecloth	Cotton	250 g	9 oz
Tea-towel	Cotton	100 g	$3\frac{1}{2}$ oz
Bath-towel	Cotton	700 g	1 lb 8 oz
Hand-towel	Cotton	350 g	12 oz
Double sheet	Cotton	500 g	1 lb 2 oz
Single sheet	Cotton	350 g	12 oz

☐ Special treatments

Handkerchiefs can be soaked overnight in cold water with a handful of salt, to dislodge clinging mucus.

Nappies as they are used can be put immediately into sterilizing solution (e.g. Napisan, or a solution of household bleach: $\frac{1}{4}$-egg cup per 4.5 litre/1 gallon of water) in a covered bucket. First scrape off solid soil and flush down the loo. Rinse and then wash at a temperature of at least 95°C on your machine's maximum wash cycle (the old wash code 1). Keep separate from other whites, to avoid infection.

Plastic pants should be washed by hand in hand-hot water – do not boil. Add a few drops of glycerine to the rinsing water to keep soft.

Pillow cases in polyester/cotton may need soaking to dislodge absorbed grease.

For badly stained items products are now available to boost the power of ordinary washing powders. These dissolve rapidly even at low temperatures releasing active oxygen which treats brown stains and ingrained dirt. For example Stain Salts.

□ **Laundrettes**

A hot wash at the laundrette is usually a maximum of 60°C, which you can use for colourfast cottons, linens, and possibly for strong nylons and coloured polyester/cottons. But the bleach in traditional heavy-duty washpowders for automatics does not work quickly until around 80°C, and for this reason extra bleach to add to an all-white wash is often available at laundrettes. It will be more efficient and economical if you take your own washing product with you. Most suitable would be one of the new heavy-duty washing liquids, which are convenient to carry and to store and are formulated to work at low temperatures. A warm wash at laundrettes is usually 40°C and you can use this for man-made fibres. Don't be tempted to overload machines: it is a false economy. Your washing will not be completely cleaned. And always remember that 'wash separately' means what it says: just one item that is not colourfast can ruin a whole load of clothes.

WASHING BY HAND

Learn to recognize immediately the symbol for hand-wash only (see page 60). Many people think that this means 'wash in hand-hot water', but it doesn't. Wool and many delicate fabrics should usually be washed by hand, as should garments which are not colourfast (see Colourfast test, below). Soaking can shift heavy soiling or stains, particularly if you use an enzyme 'biological' powder (but not for wool or silk).

In general use water that is pleasantly warm to the hand. However, if washing cottons, linens, etc. (when no machine is available), water should be as hot as possible (you can add from a boiled kettle) otherwise some washing powders cannot work properly (rubber gloves help here). If necessary, boil white cotton and linens (tea-towels or nappies) separately. Use as large a container as possible (an old tin bath is ideal). Use enough of a heavy-duty washing product to give a 5 cm (2 in) lather and boil for not longer than 10 minutes. After that, you start to re-deposit soil on the clothes.

▲ *Washing, Drying & Ironing*

Before immersing fabrics, make sure that measured amounts of washing powders are thoroughly dissolved; swish the water vigorously, a quick stir is not enough. Washing that comes in contact with undissolved powder could go patchy. Don't add pure powder without removing washing. Rinse thoroughly *at least three times* (cold water is usually adequate). Towels, etc., will be scratchy if not properly rinsed and some shower-proof finishes may lose their effectiveness. If detergent suds annoyingly won't rinse away, rub a bar of soap through them and they will vanish down the drain.

There are various common disaster areas for hand-washing: hints to avoid them follow.

□ **Colourfast test**

When colours are not 'fast' (i.e. they come out during washing) be sure to wash articles on their own, or you may spoil the rest of your washing. To test for colourfastness, dip a small, inconspicuous part of the article into warm water and iron (set iron to two dots, i.e. warm) between two clean white cloths. If traces of colour are transferred to the cloth, wash the article on its own in warm suds quickly and rinse well. Remove excess moisture by rolling in an old towel or by spinning, to prevent loose dyes collecting together to give a patchy effect. Dry flat and keep apart from other clothes till dry. Put polythene (e.g. an old carrier bag) inside multi-coloured garments which are not fast, to prevent colours from one side staining the other.

□ **Washing woollens**

Some woollens can be machine washed: look for the label. But many woollen articles must be washed by hand.

1 Wash each article separately if colourfastness is doubtful.

2 Use a gentle washing product designed especially for hand-washing, e.g. Lux flakes, Dreft, Stergene or Woolite cold water wash. *Carefully read directions on pack.* Soapless, i.e. synthetic detergents (Dreft, Stergene, Woolite), are best for hard water areas because of the problem of rinsing off scum.

3 Take measurements of garments if final shape is very important, or draw the outline of the garment onto plain paper (*not* newspaper).

4 Shake to get rid of as much loose dirt and dust as possible.

5 Do up any buttons and turn garment inside out.

6 Immerse in washing solution. Gently squeeze. Do not rub, twist or wring. 'Felting' is caused by rubbing and heat and once it happens, it cannot be corrected.

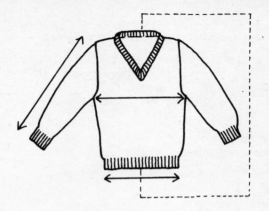

To preserve the shape and size of a jumper take the following measurements before washing: length of arms; width below armholes; width at hem; centre of neck band to hem.

7 Rinse two or three times in clear water at the same temperature as the initial wash water. Take care as you lift always to support the weight of the garment.

8 After the last rinse, do not wring. Roll in a clean towel and press well to absorb excess moisture. Alternatively, spin dry for about one minute, wrapped in a towel or washing net.

9 Dry on a flat surface away from fluorescent lighting or sun (which will yellow whites) and from any direct heat, at normal room temperature. Carefully arrange garment in correct shape (refer to measurements if taken, or use pattern). Do not stretch ribbing.

10 Correctly washed, woollens require little ironing. But you can press from the back while slightly damp with a warm iron (two dots) or when dry with warm iron under a damp cloth, or with a steam iron. Press with up-and-down action, not backwards and forwards over the garment. Do not press ribbing.

11 Always fold woollens to store, after airing well. Do not hang them up or they may stretch out of shape.

Relaxation shrinkage occurs with some new wool garments. If, during manufacture, the natural crimp in the wool fibre is stretched, it will revert back to its springy state when washed and the garment will shrink. The problem is common with hand-knitting which has been worked too tightly. To counteract this effect, you can slightly stretch the garment as it dries.

▶ *Washing, Drying & Ironing*

Cashmere (from goats) Wash as wool, but avoid rubbing at all costs. Do not let garments become too dirty. Never press.

Mohair (from goats) and angora (from goats and rabbits) Take special care with reshaping mohair items while drying flat. It is a good idea to measure (see 3, above). Do not press. Brush up pile when dry. Angora Washcreme is a unique Swiss product sold in tubes for washing delicate woollens, silk and fine fabrics.

☐ **Washing tee-shirts**

Look for the label and machine wash on programme suggested.

To hand-wash:

1 Immerse garment in a solution of warm water and washing product and squeeze. Do not soak or wring.

2 Rinse in cold water. Spin, or squeeze in a dry towel.

3 Reshape and dry flat immediately or support weight over a towel over a chair back. Never leave crumpled while damp.

4 Use a warm iron, preferably while the garment is still slightly damp.

☐ **Washing silk**

Clean or wash silk frequently; avoid heavy soiling. Test for colourfastness (see page 66) and if not, dry-clean. Dry-cleaning is also recommended for badly stained garments and the following: taffetas, chiffons, brocades, many multi-coloured prints, dressing gown fabrics, ties and scarves. As always, look for the label. Perspiration may weaken the fabric; protect under arms with pads if possible.

To hand-wash:

1 Dissolve a mild washing product in lukewarm water according to pack.

2 Immerse garment and squeeze gently. Do not soak, boil, bleach, rub or wring.

3 Rinse well, with final cold rinse.

4 Roll in towel to squeeze out excess moisture. Do not leave crumpled.

5 Dry away from sun or direct heat.

6 Press on wrong side with a warm iron. If iron is too cool, it will drag, but if it is too hot it will spoil the fabric. Press slubbed fabrics (those with raised irregular threads) and crepes and most wild or Tussore silks when dry; other silks when evenly damp. Finish off lightly on right side. Use a pressing cloth for silk with a rib or slub otherwise you may make the fabric fluffy. Do not use a steam iron. Do not redamp in parts, or the water may stain (but if this happens, dip in warm water for about 3 minutes, allow to dry and re-iron when slightly damp).

☐ **Washing acrylics**

Acrylics (Acrilan, Courtelle, and Orlon) are very common for synthetic knitted garments. Look for the label. Never use bleach and wash before the garment gets very dirty. In general acrylics can be machine washed. Use a medium wash on synthetics cycle at a temperature not exceeding 40°C. High temperatures can set creases.

To hand-wash:

1 Use warm water; do not twist or wring.

2 Use a final cold rinse to prevent creasing.

3 Roll in towel, or give a short spin (maximum 20 seconds) wrapped in a towel.

4 Dry flat. Never drip dry: this distorts the length.

5 Minimum ironing. Use a cool iron on the *back* of the fabric when it is *completely dry*. Ironing while damp (or using a steam iron) causes stretching and an ugly shine called glazing.

DRYING

The square wash code symbols relate to drying.

Means tumble-drying is the ideal method (not essential, of course). Tumble-dry synthetics at lowest possible heat – follow recommendations in machine booklet for other fabrics.

The rest of the drying symbols below are no longer in general use, but are still found on some garments.

Means drip-dry. Hangers are easiest for shirts, blouses, etc., but make sure they do not stain. Final rinse is cold.

Means dry flat – spread a towel on a table or on a rack or piece of hardboard over the bath for heavy garments.

▶ *Washing, Drying & Ironing*

IRONING

Match the dots on your iron controls to the dots on the iron symbols on the garment label, which is explained below.

☐ Ironing symbols

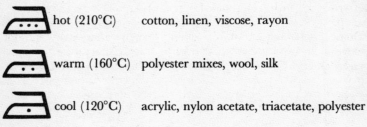

	hot (210°C)	cotton, linen, viscose, rayon
	warm (160°C)	polyester mixes, wool, silk
	cool (120°C)	acrylic, nylon acetate, triacetate, polyester
		do not iron

However, older irons may have numbers: 1 for cool, 2 for warm, 3 for medium hot, 4 for hot and 5 for very hot.

First of all look at the label on the article. If the label is missing or gives no ironing advice, look for fibre content label and refer to fibre ironing guide, above. But if you do not know what fibre it is, first use a cool setting: if creases do not come out, try a higher setting with care, testing on seam or facing before moving on carefully to iron the rest of the garment.

☐ Ironing hints

● Always iron fabrics which need the coolest setting first.

● Bear in mind that some items may have trimmings that need a cooler setting than the main fabric. If the iron is too hot, synthetics will simply melt. In this case, do not allow iron to cool, but turn to hot. Use paper to wipe soleplate clean – do not scrape. When iron is cool, gently remove small remaining traces with a soleplate cleaner, e.g. Vilene from a hardware shop or a chemist.

● Try and iron with long smooth strokes, arranging fabric so that you can cover as large an area as possible. If directions say 'press', lift iron up and down rather than running over fabric.

● Some fabrics go shiny and should be ironed from the back. These include silk, acetate and triacetates (Dicel and Tricel) and some delicate polyesters, which should be ironed when evenly damp. Acrylics should be ironed from the back *when dry* – do not use a steam iron. To prevent a shine on heavy fabrics (e.g. wools, viscose rayon, polyester/wools) use a damp cotton pressing cloth and press from the front. A well-laundered tea-towel or cotton pillow case is ideal.

● Always iron thick parts such as collars, cuffs, etc., on both sides with the wrong side first. Iron collars from point *inwards*, to avoid creases at the tip.

● Do not iron over buttons or fastenings – many irons have a button groove at their tip so that you can iron up to and round buttons. Do not iron nylon zips. Do not iron elastic or elasticated garments or ribs.

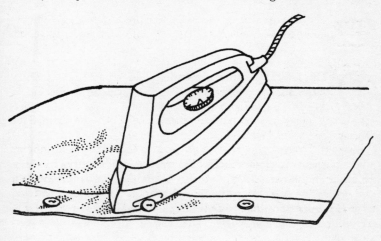

Using the button groove to iron around and between buttons.

● Never iron on the right side over seams or hems as they will leave an impression on the surface of the garment. Turn garments inside out and press up to seams and hem stitching-lines from the wrong side with a damp pressing cloth.

● Iron garments until they are dry, as garments which are still damp can be easily re-creased. Put things into airing cupboard after ironing or over a clothes rack. Don't drape over wooden chair backs unless over a towel as warmth and moisture could draw out colouring from the wood.

● After ironing hang up each garment on non-stain hangers, or fold neatly.

DRY-CLEANING

Again, as always, look for the label. The circular dry cleaning symbol is commonly misunderstood. The letters inside the circles stand for the dry-cleaning fluids to be used.

 Any solvent can be used – so you can go to any dry-cleaner or coin-op.

 Various solvents can be used; in practice you can go to any dry-cleaner or coin-op machine.

 This tells the cleaner to take certain precautions, so do not use coin-op machines.

 This indicates a special cleaning fluid for delicate fabrics or garments. Do not use a coin-op. Not even all cleaners have this. It is a good idea to draw attention to this symbol when you take in your clothes.

Some garments need very specialized treatment at the dry-cleaners – for example they may be trimmed with fur fabric, or real leather, or with sequins or feathers. Or they may be antique, or trimmed with old lace. It is important that you use a cleaner qualified to cope. If you would like the name of a dry-cleaner in your area to deal with your particular cleaning problem, contact the Association of British Launderers and Cleaners (see address list).

Never sniff at recently drycleaned clothes, and if driving home with them in the car, have at least one window open. Air clothes thoroughly before putting away. The solvents used in dry cleaning your clothes can be dangerous if you breathe them in any quantity.

□ Coin-op dry-cleaning

Do-it-yourself dry-cleaning will not be as thorough as at a professional cleaners and you must do your own pressing. Do not overload machine: this can be dangerous. Clothes with labels with the dry-cleaning circle underlined, or with letter F in the circle should not go to the coin-op (see above), neither should any quilted or padded garments, as they harbour fumes.

☐ **Sponging and pressing**

With dry-cleaning so expensive, you can resort to an old-fashioned sponge and press. Brush garment thoroughly. Treat stains as described under Stain removal, 'Dry-clean only' fabrics, page 00. Sponge with warm water plus a few drops of washing-up liquid, taking care not to overwet. Follow by a 'rinse' with a sponge well wrung-out in clear water. If woollen fabrics have gone shiny, sponge with one teaspoon of ammonia in 600 ml (1 pint) of water and follow with clean water. Allow fabric to dry before pressing, using damp cloth and using iron up and down rather than pushing along. N.B. A steam iron may only lead to shininess.

Take particular care to press trouser legs along original crease, or you will get 'tram lines'. Baggy seats and knees on woollen skirts and trousers can be laid flat on ironing board. Gather fabric together to approximate correct size. Make your cloth very damp, lay it over top and place iron down and up again quickly. With luck, the steam will shrink away the excess fabric.

SKINS AND FURS

If garments get wet allow to dry naturally on a hanger away from direct heat. Then brush as directed below. Never allow to become heavily soiled before sending to a professional cleaner recommended by the ABLC.

Always test all home cleaning methods or products on an inconspicuous part of the garment before use. Work on one skin panel at a time: don't try and tackle an area of more than 90 cm² (1 sq ft) at a time, and stick to exactly the same method throughout.

For leather coats   Follow maker's advice. Those with a shiny surface can be cleaned with a damp sponge and a solution of 1 part washing-up liquid to 5 parts warm water. Test a small area first. Leave for a minute or two then wipe over with clean damp cloth. If colour comes off, use a weaker solution. You may be able to disguise worn or scuffed areas with shoe dye.

For leather gloves   Wash gloves on the hand with Leathawash, or a solution of soap flakes (Lux). Squeeze out water from fingers down: ease lengthways and hang to dry away from direct heat or sunlight. When nearly dry work carefully on hands to restore feel and shape.

For chamois leather   Garments made or trimmed with this can usually be hand-washed using a leather shampoo. Mix a teaspoon of olive oil

▶ *Washing, Drying & Ironing*

with a cup of warm water and add to the final rinse to help soften the garment. As the garment dries, flex it from time to time with your hand to prevent stiffening.

For suede, sheepskin and pigskin   These should be gently brushed with a nail brush every three to four weeks of wear: then brush the pile up, down and sideways with a dry sponge. Protect with a suede and leather protector. Grease marks may respond to sprinkling with talcum powder; leave for an hour then brush off. Or try an all-over clean with Swade Groom cloth. Dry soil can be shifted with Swade Aid, an abrasive block sold for suede, working gently over an area considerably larger than the soiled spot. Punch market a suede renovator for shoes.

For long fur piles, use a wide-toothed comb and gently comb through against the 'fall' (natural direction' of the pile. With low piles, e.g. Persian Lamb, you can use a very soft hairbrush gently across and down the pile. For small fur items, you can try cleaning with bran which you should warm in the oven on a baking tray. Rub this into the fur and allow to cool, then brush off very thoroughly. Try warm plain flour on grubby sheepskin linings.

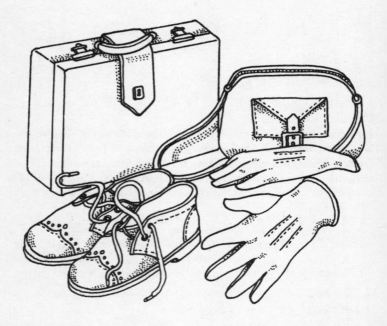

FABRIC STAIN REMOVAL

S tain removal at home is always a risky business. It is very difficult to give specific advice because of the number of variables involved: type of stain, type of fabric or furnishings and fibre, colour of fabric, age of stain and so on.

The hints on the following chart are intended only for guidance: *always test methods first on an unseen or inconspicuous part of the article before going on to tackle the stain.*

Safety First

- Keep your own stain removal kit together in one place.
- Store products/chemicals in original containers out of the reach of children; most items are poisonous. Do not empty into containers which have held food or drink.
- Many items are also very flammable, and may give off harmful fumes.
- Carry out stain removal in a well ventilated room and do not breathe any fumes.
- Do not work near a naked flame (this includes not only open coal fires, but also fires with gas or electric exposed radiants, and gas pilot lights). And do not smoke or light a match.

STAIN REMOVAL KIT AND CHEMICALS

You will find the following items useful to keep in your kit:

Clean white absorbent cloths; white tissues or roll of loo paper.

Wooden spatula (clean lolly stick), spoon or blunt knife for scraping off excess matter.

Glycerine (from a chemist). To lubricate old stains. Dilute 1 part glycerine to 2 parts water. Apply and leave for about one hour, then soak in cool suds before washing according to fibre.

Laundry borax Safe for most fibres. Make up solution of 15 ml borax to 500 ml warm water for sponging or soaking washables, method 2 and 3 below. Use the boiling water method, see method 5 below, for white fabrics.

Methylated spirit (preferably white: from a chemist or hardware shop). Use solvent method 1, see below. Do not use on acetates. Inflammable and poisonous.

White vinegar (acetic acid) from a grocer. Use 5 ml vinegar to 250 ml water, for soaking or sponging (methods 2 and 3). Do not use on acetates and keep away from skin.

Ammonia Dilute 1 part ammonia to 2 parts water. Use for sponging or soaking, see methods 2 and 3 below. Keep away from eyes and skin. Do not breathe fumes.

Acetone or amyl acetate (from a chemist) Use solvent method 1, see below. Highly flammable; buy in small quantities and if possible store outside. Nail varnish is a substitute, but most types contain oil which in itself may stain. Do not use acetone, amyl acetate or nail varnish on acetates; substitute white spirit for these fabrics.

Branded stain removal solvent Always read directions on pack. A bottle of liquid is useful (Beaucaire, Thawpit, Dabitoff): use solvent method 1, see below. In addition, buy an aerosol type (such as Goddards Dry Clean, K2r) for delicate fabrics which may ring mark with liquids. Spray on, allow to dry, brush off. In general, do not use branded solvents on rubberized or waterproofed fabrics, or on plastics, leather or silks. But read warnings on packs. They are flammable.

White spirit, turpentine and lighter fuel Apply by solvent method 1, below. Poisonous and highly flammable: store outside the house if possible.

Petrol Used for very heavy grease stains but this is highly flammable and volatile, and must be stored outside the home. Use solvent method 1 as described in the following section.

Bleaches Heavy duty washing powders contain sodium perborate bleach which is most active at temperatures above 80°C, thus washing powders will shift many stains but first always soak protein stains such as blood, gravy and perspiration in cool suds as immediate hot water will set the stain so that it becomes impossible to remove.

Household (chlorine) bleach   Cheap and easy to obtain but should only be used on white cotton or linens (without special finishes, e.g. drip-dry or flame resistant finish). Always dilute according to instructions but in general use 5 ml to 300 ml (1 teaspoon to½ pint) of water. Use method 6 and rinse well.

Hydrogen peroxide bleach   More expensive than bleach. Buy it from the chemist and ask for '20 vol' which denotes the strength. Use 1 part 20 vol to 6 parts cold water. You can use it on all fibres, but take care with coloureds as it may fade them a little. Rinse well. See method 6, below.

STAIN REMOVAL METHODS

For advice on using the methods described below to remove specific stains, refer to the stain removal chart, pages 80–81.

In all cases, first scrape off any solids with spatula; gently blot up excess liquids with clean tissues or white cloth. Always treat stains quickly – they may 'set' if left.

☐ **Method 1: Solvents**

For washable fabrics and, with caution, for non-washables. Place an absorbent pad of clean white fabric against the stain on the right side of the fabric. Take another pad of the same fabric, moisten with solvent and apply to the stain on the wrong side of the fabric, so that you are pushing the stain out the way it went in. Use the solvent as sparingly as you can. Work from the outside of the stain inwards to avoid making a 'ring'. Keep turning the pads around to present clean surfaces. Carry on until no further staining matter is being carried on to the clean dry pad. Then take a clean pad lightly moistened with solvent and lightly 'feather-out' from the centre of the stain outwards. Then wash according to the fabric.

□ **Method 2: Sponging**

For non-washable fabrics. Sometimes if you are quick you may be able to thwart a permanent stain simply by sponging. In general use cold water with just a drop of washing-up liquid added. Place pad of clean cloth under stain and with clean, barely-moisted white cloth or sponge lightly stroke the right side of the fabric. Do not use coloured paper napkins which will stain.

□ **Method 3: Soaking**

Washable fabrics only (do not soak wool, silk or non-fast colours, flame resistant or rubberized fabrics, or articles with metal fasteners). Never use hot water which will simply set the stain. Sometimes it helps first to 'lubricate' the stain by rubbing in a little glycerine solution or neat washing-up liquid. A soak in detergent solution is frequently beneficial; or you can use an enzyme washing powder designed especially for soaking – effective for protein and water-based stains which include gravy, blood, egg, tea and coffee. The colder the water the longer you must leave fabric to soak. Soak overnight in cold water, soak for 3 to 4 hours in warm water (40°C). Then wash according to the fabric.

□ **Method 4: Washing**

For washable fabrics only, of course. Look for the label. Many stains will simply wash out in good rich suds, providing you can treat them quickly. Use water as hot as the fabrics can stand, but some stains should be soaked first in cold water, see chart. If possible soak stain (or at least sponge it) until you can wash the article. A pre-wash aerosol stain-removal spray (e.g. Shout) can be helpful. Stains that usually wash out are as follows: beetroot, blackcurrant and other fruit juices, blood, chocolate, cocoa, coffee, cream, egg, gravy, iced lollies, jam, meat, tomato ketchup, washable ink, and wines and spirits. But see additional notes for some of these stains on chart, which recommends any special treatments necessary.

☐ **Method 5: Boiling water**

Only for white linens and cottons. Sprinkle stain with laundry borax and stretch article over a basin, then pour boiling water through from as high as possible. Take care not to scald yourself; wear rubber gloves if possible.

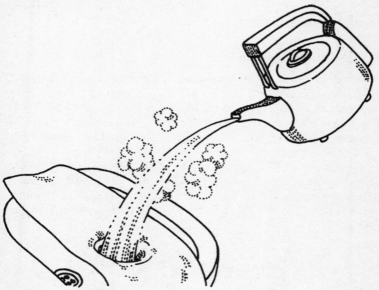

☐ **Method 6: Bleaching**

Washable fabrics only. See notes on different bleaches available under 'stain removal kit and chemicals' above. First twist the fabric around the stain to prevent the solution from spreading to the rest of the fabric and soak only stained part of article in the bleach solution. Always rinse thoroughly and use bleaches with great caution.

☐ **Method 7: Absorbent powders**

Use for greasy stains on non-washable fabrics. Dampen stain slightly and sprinkle with an absorbent powder such as french chalk or talcum powder. If fabric is likely to mark with water (e.g. satin, silk, acetates) simply hold in front of kettle spout. When powder is dry, brush off. Alternatively use an aerosol stain-removal solvent.

N.B. Stain Devils is a range of branded stain removers each formulated to remove particular stains, and widely available.

▲ *Fabric Stain Removal*

Before using this chart it is essential to read preceeding notes on methods and stain removal kit and chemicals.

Stain		Washable fabrics	Non-washable fabrics
Adhesives			Fresh stains may be lightly sponged with solvents suggested for washable fabrics; otherwise take to dry-cleaners.
	Clear adhesives	Acetone, method 1. Except for acetates: try white spirit, method 1.	
	Contact adhesive	As above.	
	Epoxy resins	Meths or white spirit, method 1, until set. Impossible to remove once set.	
	Latex adhesive	Damp cloth, until set. If set, try paint-brush cleaner, method 1, or write to manufacturer for special solvent.	
	Polystyrene (model-making) *adhesive*	Use special solvent available from model shops, method 1.	
Alcohol		Fresh stains: soak briefly in luke-warm water, method 3. Then wash, method 4. Dried stains: white fabrics, hydrogen peroxide solution, method 6. Coloured fabrics: vinegar solution, method 3. But use borax solution for acetates. Then wash, method 4.	Cool water, method 2. If stain persists take to dry-cleaners.

Spirits (gin, whisky etc.)		Sponge with clear, warm water, method 2. Then wash method 4.	Cool water, method 2. If stain persists take to dry-cleaners.
	Wine	Most fresh stains will wash out, method 4. Old stains, hydrogen peroxide bleach solution, method 3.	Cool water, method 2. If stain persists take to dry cleaners.
Ballpoint		See ink.	
Beer		See alcohol.	
Blood		Soak in *cold* water and salt or in a biological detergent, method 3. Then wash, method 4. Stubborn stains may be lubricated with glycerine then treated with hydrogen peroxide plus few drops of ammonia, method 6.	Take to dry-cleaners as soon as possible.
Butter		As for fat.	
Candlewax		Scrape off excess; or harden with ice-cube. Place stained area between blotting paper and use warm iron to melt out wax. Then use branded stain-removal solvent, method 1.	As for washable fabrics, or take to dry-cleaners.

▲ *Stain Removal Chart*

Stain	Washable fabrics	Non-washable fabrics
Car & cycle oil	Scrape off deposits, so as not to spread. Rub with neat washing-up liquid, or spray with pre-laundry aerosol, then wash at as high a temperature as fabric can stand, method 4. If fabric cannot take a high temperature use branded stain-removal solvent.	Carefully scrape off excess and take to cleaners as quickly as possible.
Carbon paper	Dab with methylated spirits; but use white spirit for acetates.	Dab cautiously with meths or white spirit; or take to dry-cleaners.
Chalks & crayon	Brush off as much as possible; then sponge with warm detergent solution; method 2 and wash. Treat any remaining traces of colour with meths.	Brush off excess and take to dry-cleaners.
Chewing gum	Harden deposits with ice-cubes, or for small items place in fridge inside a plastic bag. Crack and pick off excess with fingernail. Then apply liquid branded stain removal solvent, method 1. Finally wash, method 4.	

Chocolate	Scrape off deposits and proceed as for cocoa below.
	Remove excess; apply carpet shampoo solution followed when dry by branded stain removal solvent if necessary.
Cocoa	Blot up excess with clean cloth; soak in warm suds, method 3, then wash, method 4, preferably in biological detergent. Any difficult stains can be treated with hydrogen peroxide solution, method 6.
	Blot up excess; take to dry-cleaners as quickly as possible.
Coffee	As for cocoa above.
Cosmetics	Carefully blot up excess; try not to rub in. Apply branded stain removal solvent, followed by methylated spirits for any remaining traces of colour, method 1. Then wash, method 4.
	Blot up excess; use branded stain removal solvent cautiously or take to dry-cleaners.
Creosote and tar	Scrape off excess so as not to spread the stain. Soften with neat washing-up liquid or by rubbing in a little butter. Wash in as high temperature as fabric will stand, method 4.
	Scrape off excess very gently and take to dry-cleaners as quickly as possible.

▲ *Stain Removal Chart*

Stain	Washable fabrics	Non-washable fabrics
Egg	As for food.	
Fat, grease & oil	Scrape and blot off excess gently. Apply neat washing-up liquid, or pre-wash laundry stain-removing spray, or for delicate fabrics use eucalyptus oil then wash, method 4, in as hot water as fabric can stand. When dry use branded stain removal solvent if necessary.	Light staining can sometimes be treated with branded stain removal solvent (use aerosol/powder type for delicate fabrics, method 7). But take heavy stains to dry-cleaners.
Felt-tip pens	See ink.	
Food	Scrape off excess gently: soak fresh or dried stains in cold biological detergent solution (method 3). Or apply pre-wash aerosol stain spray. Then wash, method 4. Any remaining grease stain can be treated with branded stain-removal solvent. Treat stains from any colouring matter with hydrogen peroxide solution.	Scrape off excess gently; sponge cautiously with warm water and a few drops of washing-up liquid, method 2, or apply liquid branded stain-removal solvent, method 1 or try method 7. Or take to dry-cleaners.

Stain	Treatment	
Fruit juice	Rinse under cold tap. Soak and wash in biological detergent, methods 3 and 4. For white cotton and linen, try laundry borax, method 5. For stubborn stains, try hydrogen peroxide solution, method 6.	Sponge with a little cold water, method 2. Blot dry. Or take to dry-cleaners.
Grass	Apply methylated spirits, method 1, and soak and wash in biological detergent solution, methods 3 and 4.	You may be able to treat small stains with methylated spirits, method 1, otherwise take to dry-cleaners.
Gravy	As for food.	
Grease	See fat.	
Hair oil	As for fat.	
Hair spray	As for nail varnish.	
Handcream	As for fat.	
Ice-cream	As for food.	
Ink	Treat as quickly as possible. Blot up excess.	

continued overleaf

▲ *Stain Removal Chart*

Stain	Washable fabrics	Non-washable fabrics
Ballpoint and Biro	Do not wet. Apply methylated spirits, method 1, then wash, method 4. Take bad stains to cleaners.	Small marks may respond to methylated spirits, method 1; or take to dry-cleaners.
Felt-tip pens	If water-based, lubricate with a little washing-up liquid and wash, method 4. Otherwise apply methylated spirits, method 1, then wash, method 4.	Try methylated spirits on small stains, method 1. Otherwise take to the dry-cleaners.
Washable ink	Rinse under running cold tap. Wash in heavy duty detergent. Treat any remaining stains as for iron mould.	Take to dry-cleaners.
Permanent ink	Write to manufacturers for special advice. Or apply methylated spirits, method 1. Or try sprinkling with salt and dampening with lemon juice and leave for an hour. Rinse, then wash, method 4.	Take to dry-cleaners.
Iron mould (rust)	Apply a little lemon juice and leave for about 15 minutes; rinse and repeat if necessary. For white cottons and linens, buy rust remover. Wool/silk should be treated professionally.	Take to dry-cleaners.

Jam	As for food.
Ketchup, chutney, pickles	As for food.
Lipstick	Carefully remove any excess so as not to spread stain. Apply methylated spirits; then lubricate with a little neat washing-up liquid and wash, method 4. Take to dry-cleaners.
Marmalade	As for food.
Mascara	As for lipstick.
Mayonnaise	As for food.
Meat juice	As for blood.
Medicines	Soak in cold water, method 3 and wash, method 4. Traces of colour can be treated with methylated spirits. Any persistent greasy stains can be treated with branded stain removal solvent, method 1. You may be able to sponge small stains method 2. Otherwise take to dry-cleaners immediately.

Stain	Washable fabrics	Non-washable fabrics
Mildew	Avoid if possible. Never leave damp clothes crumpled in ironing basket, on the floor, or in cupboard. Washing several times, method 4, will remove light marks. Otherwise use chlorine bleach peroxide solution on other fabrics, method 6.	Take to dry-cleaners.
Mould	To remove light marks, wash several times, method 4. For heavy soiling, method 6.	Take to dry-cleaners
Nail varnish	Carefully scrape and blot up excess; do not spread. Apply acetone but not on acetates, method 1. You can use nail varnish remover but most types contain oils which may themselves stain. Finally wash, method 4.	Use acetones with caution, and never on acetates, method 1. Preferably take to dry-cleaners.
Oil	As for fat.	

Paint	Act immediately. Take bad stains to cleaners. Some dried marks cannot be shifted. *For water-based emulsion paints*, for example 'vinyls' – scrape off excess but do not spread, sponge at once with clear cold water (rinse under running tap if possible). Wash, method 4. Try methylated spirits on dried stains. *For oil-based 'gloss' paints* – scrape off excess without spreading, do not wash. Apply generous amounts of white spirit, method 1. Then sponge with cold clear water before washing, method 4.	Water-based emulsion – sponge off small fresh marks with damp cloth. Take large stains to dry-cleaners. Oil-based paints – treat small stains with white spirit, method 1. Take larger stains to dry-cleaners.
Perfume	If possible rinse immediately. Lubricate dried stains with glycerine before washing, method 4.	With caution, try rubbing the affected area with glycerine solution, immediately followed by sponging with a cloth which has been dampened in warm water, but take bad stains and delicate fabrics to dry-cleaners.

Stain	Washable fabrics	Non-washable fabrics
Perspiration	*Fresh stains* – dampen and hold over open bottle or small saucer of ammonia but do not breathe fumes yourself. Then wash, if possible in biological detergent, method 4. *Old stains* – sponge with vinegar solution, then soak in biological detergent solution, method 3. *Bad stains* – you can try hydrogen peroxide solution on bad stains, method 6.	Try cautiously sponging with vinegar solution, method 2, or take to dry-cleaners.
Rust	As for iron mould.	
Sauces	As for food.	
Scorch marks	Moisten with water, soften with glycerine and wash, method 4. Try bleaching heavy marks with hydrogen peroxide solution method 6, but do take care as fibres may be permanently damaged.	Take to dry-cleaners.

Shoe polish	Remove excess carefully, then apply branded stain removal solvent, method 1. Then wash, method 4.	Remove excess and take to dry-cleaners.
Soft drinks	As for fruit juice.	
Spirits	See alcohol.	
Tar	See creosote.	
Tea	As for cocoa.	
Urine	Soak in cold water, method 3, then wash method 4. Treat old stains with hydrogen peroxide solution method 6.	Take to dry-cleaners.
Vomit	Remove as much as possible with spatula. Soak in warm biological solution, with few drops of disinfectant, method 3. Then wash, method 4. If smell lingers, repeat.	Remove excess; sponge with warm water plus few drops of ammonia; or take to dry-cleaners.
Wine	See alcohol.	

▶ *Stain Removal Chart*

MANUFACTURERS' ADDRESSES

Most products are available from one of the following: grocers; supermarkets; department, hardware and DIY shops; chemists or builders' merchants.

Addresses of manufacturers of specialized hard-to-find products are listed below. In the following entries, names of products are in bold and the names of manufacturers or advice bodies are in italics. Always read directions carefully and test products on small area where relevant.

ABCLRS (The Association of British Laundry, Cleaning and Rental Services), Lancaster Gate House, 319 Pinner Road, Harrow, Middlesex HA1 4HX

Angora Washcreme, Governors Hall, High Street, Dulverton TA22 9HB

Antiquax, James Briggs Ltd, Lion Works, Old Market Street, Manchester M9 3DU

Ataka, Laboratory Facilities Ltd, 24 Britwell Road, Burnham, Slough SL1 8AG

BAL (Building Adhesives Ltd), Longton Road, Trentham, Stoke-on-Trent, ST4 8JB

A Bell & Company Ltd, Kingsthorpe, Northampton NN2 6LT

Bissell Appliances Limited, Jubilee Avenue, Highams Park, London E4 9HN

Bournseal, Cuprinol Ltd, Adderwell, Frome, Somerset BA11 1NL

James Briggs Ltd, See Antiquax

Bristol-Myers Co Ltd, Swakeleys House, Milton Road, Ickenham, Uxbridge, Middlesex UB10 8NS

The Cadogan Company Ltd, Cadogan House, 95 Scrubs Lane, London NW10 6QU

Carpet Cleaners Association, 97 Knighton Fields Road West, Leicester

Chempro, See DDD Limited

Connoisseurs Treasure Gold   119 Ladbroke Road, London W11 3PR

The Copper Shop, 48 Neal Street, London WC2H 9PA

DDD Ltd, 94 Rickmansworth Road, Watford, Herts, Herts WD1 7JJ

DIB (Drycleaning Information Bureau), Lancaster Gate House, 319 Pinner Road, Harrow, Middlesex HA1 4HX

Dylon International Ltd, Worsley Bridge Road, London SE26 5HD

J Goddard & Sons, As for Johnson Wax Ltd

Hagerty, 38 Longfield, Great Missenden, Bucks HP16 0EG

Hidelife, Bridge of Weir Ltd, Clysedale Works, Bridge of Weir, Scotland PA11 3LF

HLCC (Home Laundering Consultative Council), British Apparel Centre, 7 Swallow Place, London W1R 7AA

Impact, Soilax Limited, David Murray John Building, Swindon SN1 1ND

Johnson Wax Ltd, Frimley Green, Camberley, Surrey GU16 5AJ

Kleeneze Ltd, Martins Road, Hanham, Bristol BS15 3DY

Lever Bros Ltd, Lever House, St James's Road, Kingston-upon-Thames, Surrey KT1 2BA

Liberon, 6 Park Street, Lydd, Kent TN29 9AY

Liftoff, Celmec Ltd, Victoria Works, Saxon Street, Denton, Manchester M34 3AJB

Magic Touch, Grants Products International Ltd, 5 Lancaster Road, Worthing, West Sussex BN12 4BP

Mr Muscle, See Bristol-Myers

Minky Home Care Products, Vale Mill (Rochdale) Limited, John Street, Rochdale OL16 1HR

Movol, See Dylon

Nairn Information Service, Old Loom House, Back Church Lane, London E1 1LS

Oust, See Dylon

Oz, See Dylon

Prestige Group plc, Prestige House, 14–18 High Holborn, London EC1 2LQ

Proctor & Gamble Ltd, PO Box 1EL, City Road, Newcastle upon Tyne NE99 1EL

Punch Sales Ltd, Lower Farm Road, Moulton Park, Northampton NN3 1XF

Reckitt Products, Household & Toiletries Division, Stoneferry Road, Hull

Runaway, See Dylon

Rustins Ltd, Waterloo Road, Cricklewood, London NW2 7TX

Scalefree, See DDD

ServiceMaster Ltd, 50 Commercial Square, Freeman's Common, Leicester LE2 7SR

Silver Plating Formula, Anthony Green & Co., Linton House, 39/51 Highgate Road, London NW5 1TL

Silver Solution, Sheffco Ltd, 70–78 York Way, London N1 9AG

Simply White, See Dylon

Stain Salts, See DDD

Swade Products, Orkin of London Ltd, 7 Wembley Park Business Centre, North End Road, Wembley, Middlesex HA9 0AS

Topps, TJR Ltd, Capital House, 662 London Road, North Cheam, Sutton, Surrey SM3 9BY

Vilene, Vileda Ltd, PO Box 3, Ellistones Lane, Greatland, Halifax, West Yorkshire HX4 8NJ

Vitreous Enamel Development Council Ltd, New House, High Street, Ticehurst, Wadhurst, Sussex

Wendol, Hohn & Hohn, Haan, West Germany

Zebrite, See Reckitt

INDEX